DO YOU HAVE A MOMENT?

DO YOU HAVE A MOMENT?

50 Spiritual Posts to Open and Close the Day

ROBERT J. WICKS

Paulist Press
New York / Mahwah, NJ

Cover design by Joe Galagher
Book design by Lynn Else

Library of Congress Cataloging-in-Publication Data
Names: Wicks, Robert J., author.
Title: "Do you have a moment"? : 50 spiritual posts to open and close the day / Robert J. Wicks.
Description: New York/Mahwah , NJ : Paulist Press, [2022] | Summary: "Do You Have a Moment?" offers a glimpse of lived spirituality from the author's perspective as he has encountered the circle of God's grace in his own life and shared it with others on the way...for a moment, here and there"— Provided by publisher.
Identifiers: LCCN 2021032134 (print) | LCCN 2021032135 (ebook) | ISBN 9780809155767 (paperback) | ISBN 9781587689758 (ebook)
Subjects: LCSH: Meditations.
Classification: LCC BL624.2 .W53 2022 (print) | LCC BL624.2 (ebook) | DDC 242/.2—dc23
LC record available at https://lccn.loc.gov/2021032134
LC ebook record available at https://lccn.loc.gov/2021032135

ISBN 978-0-8091-5576-7 (paperback)
ISBN 978-1-58768-975-8 (e-book)

Published by Paulist Press
997 Macarthur Boulevard
Mahwah, New Jersey 07430
www.paulistpress.com

Printed and bound in the
United States of America

On my daughter Michaele's first day of second grade in a new school, she felt she needed a friend. We had recently moved into the area, so she didn't know all the other children from the past year. She looked around the classroom and watched the other children for a while and decided a little girl named Stephanie would be the perfect friend, but she had to figure out how to meet her. And so, since each child had a designated hook for their coats, she switched Stephanie's with hers and then told her later, "I think your coat is on my hook." Stephanie was surprised because she was sure she had put hers on the right one. When she looked and saw the mistake, she apologized and that started a friendship lasting until now. Steph has just turned fifty.

I dedicate this book to **Stephanie DePaolantonio** as a reminder that she will always be part of our family and we are all grateful she believed she had put her coat on the wrong hook all those years ago.

If you get tired, learn to rest, not to quit.

— Bansky

You can't go back and change the beginning, but you can start where you are and change the ending.

— C.S. Lewis

Contents

Introduction
A Walk by the River Together...*with* God
3

. . . .

Prologue
~ Experiencing "Spiritual Moments" ~
7

....

Epilogue
~ Gifting Our Inner Silent World ~
153

....

Appendix
Experiences

....

About the Author

Introduction

A Walk by the River
Together...*with* God

> The purpose of a pilgrimage is primarily to
> create conditions within ourselves that will
> make us receptive to the light, to the images
> of the Holy Spirit.

> — Father Maximos[*]

In Sacred Scripture we are told that the first truly
spiritual experience is walking alongside God in the
garden. Looking back at my own walks alongside the
Shenandoah River in Berryville, Virginia, with my spiritual mentor, Flavian Burns, I now see it as a reenact-
ment of the Genesis story.

Burns, who was Thomas Merton's final abbot, and
I would talk about many things; it was very unstruc-
tured. At times I would wonder what was being
accomplished. However, after leaving there, I felt and
thought differently. A chance remark made, an emotion arisen, or an idea given new air seemed to make

---

[*] As quoted in Kyriacos C. Markides, *Gifts of the Desert* (New York:
Doubleday, 2005), 51.

all the difference in my understanding of how I felt God wanted me to greatly enjoy, deeply feel, and freely share the life given me.

Today, ongoing hour-long encounters such as I had with the abbot are hard to come by for most of us. Instead, I have found that rather than persons seeking me out for this type of relationship, they turn to me seeking a brief interaction. After a presentation or when encountering someone who has read my work, it is not unusual to be asked, "Do you have a moment?" Usually, since I have built in time for such brief meetings, I am able to respond, "Yes, I do. How may I help you?"

The following brief reflections are modeled after such encounters in the spirit of my walks with Father Flavian. They are very brief reflections written in a conversational style...as if we were walking along the Shenandoah River together...*with* God. My hope is that you will read only one or possibly two of the posts each day as part of a personal at-home retreat.

There is no rush to finish going through these spiritual jottings. As a matter of fact, the space you take between them may be of more import than the minute or so it takes to read each one. As you let them sit with you at the beginning of your day or before you go to bed at night (or at both times), you have a chance to let them spark your own reverie, which, in the end, may not even be the points highlighted in the reflection. After all, it is *your* "pilgrimage," so I want this to be *your* book.

Even beyond this, I believe that while I have come to write these spiritual themes on living life with certain goals in mind and you have come to open these pages with your aims, God may have different reasons in mind. If you are open to them, then theonomy (God's will) and autonomy (your will) can be joined in new, possibly deeper, ways. While at times the result may be challenging, in the end, it will always bring greater joy and inner peace. That is God's promise to us when we discern with an open, loving heart.

Thank you in advance for inviting me to walk with you. I hope as you go through the following daily reflections as a way of having a personal silent retreat at home, you will find that what you read doesn't fail you. You will know either way in how your feelings, thoughts, ways of understanding, and behavior change. Those will be the ultimate measure of what I have done, how you have chosen to respond, and how both of us were truly open to God.

Prologue

~ *Experiencing "Spiritual Moments"* ~

Spirituality opens us up to experience the truth about ourselves, others, and God. The more we can fathom who we are, the more we will appreciate the mystery of God. The more we can fathom a deeper sense of God, the more we will understand not only a richer sense of who we are but also *who we might become at any age*. Moreover, such a more encompassing sense of self and God allows us to appreciate a "circle of grace" when we interact with others. When we have the type of spiritual sense in place to allow compassion to be more natural, while expecting nothing in return, we also become aware of what and where God is calling us in the reactions of those we walk with in life. And so, open your heart as much as you can in taking out a spiritual moment or two each day to read, reflect, and pray over the following reflections. Be aware of the temptation to minimize the following lessons, ignore them, or claim they are irrelevant to you. Also, note the dead-end attitudes of arrogance (projecting the blame onto others), ignorance (the temptation to blame yourself inordinately for past mistakes), and discouragement (feeling you just can't grow and deepen) so you can avoid them. Instead, be *intrigued* as to how the psychological and spiritual themes are calling you to live more richly, compassionately, genuinely, and do what you can in response…and let God take care of the residue. There is such a gift as grace, you know.

1

A Turning Point…No Choice
Response…A Choice

And I saw the river over which every soul
   must pass
to reach the kingdom of heaven
and the name of that river was suffering;
and I saw a boat which carries souls
   across the river
and the name of that boat was love.

— St. John of the Cross

A number of years ago, I was teaching a capstone course for new psychotherapists. Part of the requirements was writing a paper that included biographical information. When I read one written by a woman in the class, I actually had to stop to let it sink in.

As life would have it, when I arrived a bit early for the next class, the woman who wrote it had also arrived early and was the only one there. As usual, she was smiling in a way that always struck me as welcoming and healing.

I sat down next to her and said, "I don't know quite how to put this but is what you wrote in your paper about your life true?"

She seemed caught by the question, as I expected she would, and replied, "Of course, why?"

"Well," I replied, "you always seem so joyous, gracious, and filled with interest in others. Yet, in your biographical section you wrote that your husband died early in the marriage leaving you with two boys to raise. One subsequently died as a young adult in a car crash and the other committed suicide a few years after that. How can you be the way you are now given all you have been through?"

The expression on her face changed at that point, she bowed her head slightly, and her smile became a wan one. After a moment of silence, she looked up and said, "It wasn't easy. It also certainly wasn't immediate. I needed to grieve each loss. I was also dumbfounded and thought, 'Why was I dealt this terrible hand—three times?' Finally, I realized that each was a turning point that I had no control over. Yet, in the end, I did have something to say about how I responded. I had *a choice*."

She went on to say, "The question for me was, Would I make the best response for myself and those who would cross my path down the road? Furthermore, could I be a special healing presence to others because of what I went through—not merely in spite of it—or would I simply remain bitter, lost, or needy for the rest of my life? The choice was mine."

I could see she was truly a remarkable woman. At that moment she taught me a lesson that could have come only from someone who had gone through so much and used it for the remainder of her life in the service of others…and to bring a special sense of life to herself as well.

Her words have never left me as I face limitations from my own suffering and past losses, societal problems from events like the COVID-19 pandemic, and surprising stresses and hurts that come my way. *I have a choice*: Will I learn to love again in new, deeper ways or will I take another path?

The question for me each time will be, Do I pick the best one for me and the world or will I hold on to, rather than honor, the past in ways that will prevent me from being present in a healing, hopeful way for the remainder of my life? It is certainly an important question…and one that *all* of us must face at different points in our lives.

What turning points are you at in your life right now? What choices are available for you to take and what help do you need to ensure you will pick a healthy one?

2

What Empties the Cup?

When you talk, you are only repeating what
you already know. But if you listen, you may
learn something new.

— Dalai Lama

Years ago when I went for spiritual mentoring, I was
presented with a statement and then asked a question to ponder. The statement was, If you feel that you
are psychologically and spiritually free, you are lost.
The question was, Can you empty your cup of what is
in you from the past in order to receive new, fresh wisdom that is helpful for you and others *now*?

Initially I was both puzzled and, I think, a bit
insulted by this opening gambit by my guide. However,
since he was the mentor, I just nodded, with the idea of
reflecting on it during the ride home. After a few days,
I realized that the main reason I sought mentoring was
to walk with someone wiser than myself. And so, I proceeded to entertain what he said more deeply.

When I returned to see him again, I had questions
to ask about it. First, I asked him, "How will I know

that I am not free inside?" He smiled, nodded, and said in reply, "You will experience negative emotions when you are dealing with certain issues or persons. In addition, you will not really be open to *listening* to something new when you ask a question of them. Instead, you will simply be looking for where their argument is weak. In essence, while you are quietly doing this, you won't be listening to learn but simply *hearing* them out, waiting for your opportunity to speak…and argue your point."

That made sense to me so I asked further, "This may seem like a foolish question, but if I accept that I am not free inside and the information I have taken in is not balanced, how do I empty myself of my opinions and rigid beliefs since I have such a big ego?"

"Ah, but that is one of the most important questions you can ask of yourself," he replied. "It is one that you must constantly ask so your ego is not so large that it is impossible to learn and there is no freedom to *unlearn*."

He then went on: "If you wish to empty yourself, you can do it by realizing that an attitude of love and charity will empty you. You will know this is happening because you will cease to argue, be sarcastic, be defensive, and be too sure of yourself. Love and charity are the portals to humility. Being sure of yourself is simply defensiveness hidden under a cloak of pride."

I was to learn these lessons *again* and *again*, because I have such a large ego and a tendency to be defensive. Yet, I realized after a while that when you take humility and add it to knowledge, you get wisdom. Then, when you take that very wisdom and add it to compassion, you get love. And love is at the heart of life. Moreover, for those of us who say we are "religious," God is love... and so if we wish to model ourselves after the divine image, we ought to *act* that way, not simply proclaim the Word from our mouths or wave the Bible in the air and feel we are in the right.

3

Spiritual Leanings

Sometimes we expect too much
and it is unfair.

We forget love
and settle for law.

We judge and fail
to remember people's suffering...

...and tough situations
and stress—especially when we are
   convinced we are right.

If we are male
we miss the female calling...

...and think we know best
rather than see the chance to learn.

If we are female
we miss the chance to know...

...males have a special gift
but it takes them longer to offer it.

Then at a special turning point
we see the Light and it is humility

that is added to knowledge
leading to wisdom…and love.

And when we lean into love,
we stop judging others

and see that the cloak of hate
    and divisiveness
covers fear and causes danger

which makes us ask:
How am I contributing to this?

How am I failing to honor:

- women who have been hurt?
- children who have been taken
  advantage of?
- the world we have been given but are
  abusing?
- the chance to bring people together?
- the opportunity to care for people who
  are ill?
- the chance to remember poor people?
- the need to welcome strangers?
- the opportunity to be a beacon of
  hope?

May I lean into love…and not judgment and
  law.
That is all I ask…even though it will make
  me feel weak…

…make me feel uncertain
and leave me dependent rather than sure.

Yes, let me lean into the messiness of life
and even though I can't see You…know You
  are there.

4

A Bridge to Heaven
…Take It!

Several months ago I noticed that when I voiced my negative opinion about a person I knew, a couple of my friends would disagree in a way that made me feel I was being too harsh or judgmental. When this happened more than once, I thought, "They have changed. Maybe I should simply keep my thoughts to myself."

Then, while in a quiet meditative moment early in the morning at church, a surprising and quite unusual thought came to me. It made me open my eyes, sit up straight, and smile…almost laugh, really. The thought was this: "We can die at any time. It doesn't matter if we are young or old. If, however, we are up in years—as I am—it is more apt to happen sooner rather than later. Wouldn't we rather meet the Lord after having been a gentle presence to someone or having said something that showed we understood the person's complex and stressful situation rather than judging them?"

I realized even more deeply at that moment that a gentle understanding attitude toward even those who malign us is certainly a "bridge to heaven." I think being that way even gives us the chance to sample heaven *now*.

However, being a realist, I also knew there is a cost to such an attitude and way of living. It is *personal vulnerability*. We feel things more deeply. And it didn't take me long to realize this.

Later that day, during the run up to an election, I received a recorded telephone call from a religious organization telling me to vote for a candidate who spewed venom and lived in a narcissistic, hedonistic, and sometimes cruel way. Since I know the organization's single-minded agenda, normally I would simply shrug it off with the thought, "Well, what do you expect?" Instead, in response, I became sad. *Very* sad.

Following this, someone whom I don't know referred to Pope Francis on Facebook as the "anti-Christ." It was because Francis said we should love and respect everyone. My reaction? Instead of feeling sorry for the person because of her own problems, rigidity, and neediness, I had to take out time to reflect and debrief myself so I wouldn't be blanketed by the last home of the ego: discouragement.

Yes, there is a true cost for being gentle.

Yet, if we saw a bridge to heaven and it was called "kindness and understanding," wouldn't we be foolish not to take it…whatever the cost? Gentleness is not weakness or soppy submissiveness. Kindness at times can also seem to be a fool's errand, but we must remember that it is also *God's* errand…and that is the most important element of all.

If "angels" in our midst encourage us to add joy and peace to the spiritual atmosphere around us, why not do it rather than talk negatively about others? Because of this approach, it is true that the hurt may feel even more crushing at times, for being on the bridge with the Lord will still not take away the pain we may feel.

Yet isn't it all worth it despite this? The transition to meeting God someday will be much easier if we live more gently now. (Also, if we approach life in a kinder way, those "angels" in our midst won't keep reminding us that we are being so critical of others.)

5

Get Out…and Stay Out!

Novelist Henry James once advised, "Get out of yourself…and stay out." I think this is good mental health advice in general but especially during these uncertain times.

Even those—maybe *especially* those—who have had a tough time early in life find that once they have taken the needed time and space to heal, a final important step in the process of living a rich and rewarding life is to become involved in compassionate activities, to make their world larger.

If you take a spoon of salt and put it in a small glass, you will taste the bitterness of the salt in the water. Put it in a lake, and you won't be able to tell the difference.

People who get overly self-involved—or by extension with their immediate circle of friends or family—and avoid activities that bring them in touch with the needs of the larger community run the risk of experiencing a "salt in a small glass experience" in their lives and attribute it to early childhood experiences. Others who reach out can actually become deeper as persons as a result of similar negative encounters in ways that would not have been possible had the trauma not happened in the first place. It is called today posttraumatic growth (PTG).

Once I was walking with two friends, one who was always self-concerned and the other a person who traveled the world with a relief organization. The first started complaining about something a neighbor was doing and then her daughter. The second, well-traveled friend smiled, looked at her, and said, "Sounds like you are having some 'first-world problems.'"

Gandhi was once praised for what he had done for India. His response was simple and telling: "I didn't do all this for India. I did it for myself." The recently deceased Supreme Court Justice Ruth Bader Ginsburg echoed this theme in a slightly different way: "If you want to be a true professional, you will do something outside yourself, something to repair tears in your community, something to make life a little better for people less fortunate than you. That's what I think a meaningful life is—living not for oneself, but for one's community."

Bottom line: get out of yourself…and stay out. Paradoxically, in doing this, *you* will feel better while helping someone outside of your interpersonal network.

6

Hope Is a Long Game... Conversations with Discouragement

Recently, a number of persons expressed to me their discouragement at the current societal, religious, and political situation:

- Don't people realize how difficult it is to be a police officer?
- Why would people vote for someone who abuses women, makes fun of the military who experienced traumatic brain injury, is only into his own ego, and is creating a fascist state?
- Shouldn't we put the abortion issue first and forget the rest for now?
- Doesn't anyone care about the clean air and water acts or the deficit we are passing on to our children and grandchildren?

- Why don't we respect the Constitutional right to carry arms as the National Rifle Association is defending?
- How would you feel and react if you saw an officer of the law kneeling on the neck of your child while he gasped for air until he died?
- Shouldn't we have educational, religious, and political leaders who respect disabled persons and those who are different than we are and want health care for poor people?
- How can anyone complain that young people aren't attracted to organized religion if women are not treated equally and religious leaders are telling us how we should vote?

However, hope is a long game. It recognizes that discouragement is one of the last homes of the ego and that it is not about us but about being faithful to what we believe is good. We must believe that if we stand for what is good and demonstrate that with a spirit of love rather than hate and divisiveness, it will prevail.

We must also take our responsibility for the failure to bring people together in a way that cares for others. Recently, someone whom I respect posted something that I felt encouraged a failure to recognize the needs of poor people. Whose fault was it? Mine. I needed to do more to bring those needs to the attention of others in a clearer fashion. Then a relative of mine posted something with the photo of Barack Obama on a toilet paper roll and thought it was funny. Whose problem was that? Mine. I had let him down because in making my point of view I did it in a way that my ego was the issue...not the truth, not kindness, not love...but my ego and desire for immediate gratification of my desire for what I believed was good.

Hope is a long game. Hope recognizes that discouragement is the last home of egoistical thinking, and hope is something that recognizes it is not all about us...others are involved...God is involved. We need to do what we can and let other good souls and God take care of the residue.

7

The Dangers of "Spiritual and Psychological Cortisone"

During these strange and tough times, there are many who feel the country is in a terrible situation because of racial tensions, a sense of divisiveness, and confusion by some as to the difference between patriotism, which is good, and nationalism, which is dangerous and destructive to the American dream.

Yet, actually, this is a natural phase in the development of a continually healthier nation and the inclusion of all its citizens—no matter their gender, skin color, or religion. It is also a predictable and necessary phase for religious groups who claim that God is love, and it is this virtue that is at the heart of what they believe and how they act toward others—whether members of their faith tradition or not.

The "good old days" were ones that often seemed that way to those in power and in possession of most of the control and money because "spiritual and psychological cortisone" covered up the ills that needed to be faced and healed. However, you can't treat what you don't see.

In today's climate, those evils have been uncovered. They are out in the open because they have been encouraged by some political and religious leaders.

Physically, cortisone can be used only for a period of time so as not to continually mask what must be treated. If such ills go unrecognized, they can develop into something more serious—and *permanent*. The same can be said of countries and faith traditions. If religions look only inward and have power and control as their watchwords, they will cease to be dynamic rivers of faith to refresh their own members, poor people, immigrants, and people who are physically ill. Likewise, if countries look only inward, the doctrines that passionately encouraged freedom and possibility will become just papers with meaningless words written on them.

Young people often recognize this and turn from nationalism that tries to cloak itself in the flag of patriotism and religions that say nice words from their Scriptures but use them to excuse such behaviors as prejudice, misogyny, a failure to protect the world from pollution in the name of immediate financial gain, and even idol worship in lieu of facing the challenges of a loving dynamic God...who loves *everyone*.

And so, these are tough, tough times. That is for sure. Without them, however, the evils in society remain hidden. People's spirits atrophy. Chronic niceness masquerades as true acceptance. When this happens, the love of our nation fails to seek to surface the challenges that need to be faced so the country can be even more faith-filled, rather than marked by self-centeredness and religiosity.

Now is the time to take advantage of what we see, not pull back, dig in our heels, or seek to run away. What Carl Jung once said about people is true about countries and religious traditions. Namely: "The brighter the light…the deeper the darkness." We now have a chance as individuals, as communities, as religious traditions, and as an entire nation to embrace the darkness and seek new light to call us forward together. What an opportunity! If we seize it we will be better as individuals and a nation. We will also embrace what is truly *spiritual* in our lives rather than be led or discouraged by secular goals.

8

Each Day

Before I am fully awake
I sit on the edge of my bed

and set goals that are high
and worthy.

And each day,
I fail in reaching them,

let myself down,
and others as well.

But each day
I still keep my eyes wide open,

don't run away,
or play down my faults.

And, each day, in return, I am surprised
by other lessons learned

that I didn't expect
…and certainly didn't deserve!

Yes, each day
has its own unforeseen awakenings

if only we take the time to look
with a renewed sense of hope...*each* day.

9

A Simple Powerful Sense of Presence…*Yours!*

Kindness frees us from the cruelty that at
times infects human relationships, from the
anxiety that prevents us from thinking of
others, from the frantic flurry of activity that
forgets that others also have a right to be
happy.

— Pope Francis

Many years ago I was on the part-time staff of a hospital in Amish Country, in Lancaster, Pennsylvania, and would make rounds for the Psychiatry Department on Sundays. It was a very busy time in my life with a clinical practice, full-time teaching, and weekly clinic patients, so I was thrilled when I thought that one week I would have a day off from this. However, just as I sat down with a cup of coffee and the Sunday newspaper, the phone rang. It was the chief of psychiatry to tell me that I was wrong and to get a certain part of my anatomy out there *immediately*. (He didn't use very psychiatric terms to make his point.)

When I got on the road, I thought that since it was Sunday I probably would be able to get to the hospital quite quickly. Instead, as I got on the single-laned Lincoln Highway (oldest U.S. highway), I saw that dreaded orange triangle up ahead on the back of an Amish buggy. I thought, "Well, he probably is only going a short distance." Instead, I followed him all the way to the doctor's parking lot.

As I ran up the stairs I wondered how busy I would be and discovered only two cases. *Yessss!* In the first room I went into there was a little Amish boy who looked bewildered and scared. The buggy he was in was hit by a car, and he was a bit traumatized by the accident and the fact that he didn't know anyone around him in the hospital. I sat down and did most of the talking and tried to calm him a bit. Finally, as I was leaving I said, "I'll come back and see you before I leave the hospital." He just nodded.

After seeing the other patient in intensive care and answering some questions from the nurses, I rushed down to my car because I had forgotten about the little boy. Finally, as I was unlocking the car door, I remembered the little Amish boy I had seen. For a few seconds I thought, "Oh, he won't remember. I can just go and return to my newspaper and a fresh cup of coffee." However, I knew that if I did, I would be thinking about him for the rest of the day and probably longer. And so, I closed and locked the car door and went back into the hospital.

As I walked into his room, I said, "Bet you thought I forgot you." Seeing a familiar face for the first time since he had been hospitalized, he looked up, gave me a wan smile, and said in a soft voice, "No, I *knew* you would remember."

At one point in 2020, with a worldwide pandemic raging, wildfires roaring in the western states, and the most divisive U.S. election I have experienced in my lifetime underway, the temptation was to think only in big terms as to what would make life better for all of us. Yet, it is often a simple smile, a nod of understanding, or a kind word that can change life for the better for those you meet in passing. Never underestimate the power of a few kind words or a smile…and never drive to rural Lancaster, Pennsylvania, behind a horse-drawn buggy if you're in a hurry.

10

Ask the Right Questions

There are two ways to be fooled. One is to
believe what isn't true; the other is to refuse
to believe what is true.

— Søren Kierkegaard

When life gets difficult, we naturally look for the
sources of our problems. Sometimes, as in the case
of a drawn-out crisis like a pandemic or other horrible
societal or personal events, there are no ready answers.
Yet, even those dire circumstances present opportunities for healthy responses.

If America is capable of horrible injustices encouraged by intelligent bad souls, it is also able to respond
in helpful, creative, and brilliant new ways by those
numerous wise persons seeking good among us.

In times of global health problems, political divisiveness, and personal failings, hopeful persons ask the
following:

- In response to my difficulties of late, what
new wisdom have I gained that is helpful

only for the present and what do I want to take with me for a lifetime?

- If and when things settle down in my country, the world, and my personal life, what should I welcome back from before the tragedies I have experienced and what should I let slip from my grip forever when a so-called new normal arrives?
- In response to the negativity around me, what can I do not to add to it but to respond with concrete acts of love?
- As I see destructive responses by groups to whom I belong, as well as by me at times, how can I learn ways to encourage care instead of projecting blame— especially when dark times occur?
- How can I remind myself that acts of love are not simply fluff and that acts of anger and discouragement are *not* more real or present in this world than caring and love are?

As I reflect on these tough questions, I remember a man responding to a rabbi who had assigned him a quite challenging task. The man said to the rabbi, "What you ask of me is very hard." The rabbi's response? He said, "I didn't know you had made a pact with God for an easy life."

The call now is simple: do what you can for others, take time to reflect and renew, and, please, stop making trouble for yourself.

11

The Spiritual Teachers around Us ...That We Miss

In a course I was leading on integrating psychology and spirituality, I once observed an unspoken reaction by one student toward another. One of the students was a Christian evangelical from a small parish in inner-city Baltimore. She sat in one of the back few rows of the classroom and was an outspoken, passionate, and even physically demonstrative person when she was experiencing anger. The second student was a quiet, somewhat reserved Buddhist who had a great deal of counseling experience and seemed ready for a next step both spiritually and psychologically. I was curious whether an opportunity would arise during the course for me to encourage this.

When the passionate student would share a feeling or stridently make a point, the quiet student would make a face. Since he sat in the front row, the other student couldn't see his reactions to her outbursts of emotion. I, however, could easily notice them but didn't say anything to him since I felt the timing wasn't quite right. Finally, when the passionate student got so worked up about an issue we were discussing in one class that she threw something at the blackboard in the front of the room and just missed my head, I knew the time had come—for *both* of them!

Later that day the student who threw her pen at the board came up to me to apologize and said, "I was over the top in my reaction. Is there something I can do about my emotions?" I replied, "They are a great gift. Why not get some short-term counseling on how to prune them? Jesus spoke about pruning, didn't he? When you prune something, it doesn't blossom less. It blossoms more deeply. It will be an even better gift not only for you to have but also to those around you." She did and it helped her focus her deep feelings in a more productive way.

In the case of the Buddhist student, right after the class when the object was thrown at the board and the expression on his face showed the greatest displeasure, I quietly asked him if he would stay a moment after everyone had left. He nodded that he would.

Once we were alone, I whispered to him as he stood up, "*She* is your spiritual mentor." He looked back at me in surprise and said, "I'll certainly have to think about that!"

"No," I replied calmly. "I didn't ask you to think about it. *She* is your spiritual mentor. This is not something to think about. It is something to practice. She can be a powerful spiritual guide for you if you let her be. She has much to teach you about yourself, and about how and why you react the way you do." Having said that to him, before he could reply or argue the point further, I smiled and abruptly left the room. He needed the time and space with himself and not with me.

The Dalai Lama once said that he learned a great deal from those who differed with him in views or style or even did not like him very much. They would tell him things others would not, and he benefited from their insights. So should we when we encounter people that we find difficult in our lives. The question remains: *Will* we...especially during turbulent religious, political, and societal times?

12

Painful Joy

I have often advised psychotherapists in training that, in the short run, their efforts to help a person to achieve greater psychological health may not work. With such patients, the therapist's health is no immediate match for the psychopathology of their patients. This is especially true in the case of persons who are diagnosed with a borderline personality. Such individuals are usually quite bright and divide people into "bad" and "good" categories depending on whether they meet their needs in the way *they* want them to. Such needy and self-destructive persons have experienced very tough times early in life and spend the rest of it, if there is no therapeutic intervention, seeking to make others feel just as terrible as they do, unless they meet their insatiable needs. And so, the therapist must be patient and focus on the "long game."

Once when I chatted with a clinical supervisor about my own hurtful encounter with a borderline patient, he laughed. This was wonderful because it broke the spell of my feeling hopeless, vulnerable, and terrible due to the hold the patient had on me because I cared and was failing. I asked, "What are you laughing about?" He then got serious and said, "Such patients need to find out that we know they are in pain, but *they* must change if they wish to be happier and more genuinely compassionate in life. Unfortunately, this is very difficult and scary for them. The broader problem is that they inflict their 'carefully aimed hurt' not simply on a trained psychotherapist but also on their friends and family."

No family is free from this. I certainly can attest to this. I must admit that because I have such a large ego I was surprised when someone close to me sought to take advantage of my wish to be helpful. When it happened, I was thrown off my game. I shared with a friend, "How could he do this to me?" The reply my friend gave was one I would have given. He said, "Well, when you hurt that much, you can't see your own role in it. It would be too debilitating. And so, you see an enemy outside of yourself and you pick someone you feel you can hurt the most because you are aware of their vulnerable points. I am sorry for him because he will continue through life thinking he has been treated poorly when, in fact, while this may have been the case earlier in life, he has cut himself off from the very people who care."

He then added a comment that surprised me. He said, "On the positive side, though, he has poked a hole in your feeling of being a totally compassionate person. That is good, even though it hurts, because it encourages greater self-awareness and humility and fosters looking at the motivations behind your caring nature. If you let it teach you, then you will be able to embrace your self-serving desires to help others. Also, it will wake you up to the fact that you don't have the luxury of giving away your joy to such persons, even though they are suffering."

I asked, "Why? What is the wake-up call?" He responded, "You will realize that this is not simply about you. You can't afford to waste energy on those who would not benefit from it because there are so many others in your life who desperately need that attention."

"Well, what about him?" I asked.

"Ah, that is a worthy question. He will either wake up or the friendship of others will provide the 'emotional cortisone' you and I often speak about that will make him feel justified and comfortable in the present. With some people, that is all that can be done, given the psychological problems they have experienced early in life."

The lesson: There are experiences that are personally painful, but if we understand and deal with them correctly, they can lead to joy, which is not only personally experienced as we feel the freedom from the need to be everything for everyone but also opens up energy for those who truly seek and benefit from our presence and attention.

13

Becoming Kinder to Your Memories …It Makes a Difference in Life

Many people don't honor their memories in a helpful, healing way, and it can be costly to how they feel and live now.

Some seek to forget their memories. That sounds good—"Let bygones be bygones" is the saying. However, it doesn't usually work that way. The only memory that will hurt you is the one forgotten because of its being pushed down into unconsciousness where it remains and operates *sub rosa*, beyond our awareness. You can see this happening when persons you barely know treat you in certain negative ways. Why are they doing that? They are transferring onto you what has happened to them in the past from someone you remind them of now. Because they are not in touch with such memories, this dysfunctional behavior results in hurting others and, really, in the end, depriving themselves of new healthy relationships and enjoyable interactions as well.

Still other people seek to be very clear about the past but are not gentle with themselves. This can lead to the person beating themselves up. Their memories become constant reminders of their failures. In response, they can react in two very different ways: one, be very hard on themselves or, two, be quite defensive. Neither provides insight, just a strange sort of immediate relief.

Sometimes memories may also lead to broader destructive tactics when recollections of past events are not treated both kindly *and* as a way of seeking insight. The result? People admire and emulate public figures from entertainment and politics who display bad behavior.

Treating your memories in a kinder way is also not tantamount to forgetting, justifying, or minimizing them. It is simply embracing them as you would a small child who is hurt and saying, "You are human. Sometimes we make mistakes or are treated terribly. The consequences are tough enough. Please don't add to them but instead learn from them…and then move forward." Remember, guilt pulls us into the past and leaves us there, whereas remorse helps us see our memories just as clearly but also helps us gain the wisdom to live our life more fruitfully in the present and future.

An added nice thing about being both clear and kind to your memories is that it opens up greater inner space to be more compassionate to others. We frown a bit less, smile a bit more, live more wisely, and help others in the process as well. Many of the good and wise people we know have learned this, and they are worth emulating. It is not that they don't have bad memories of what has been done to them or what they have done. It is that they have let those very memories teach them in ways that soften their inner spirit and enhance their generosity with others. Sounds like something we should consider worth emulating.

14

An Expensive
Mental Rental

Self-control is strength. Calmness is mastery.
You have to get to a point where your mood
doesn't shift based on the insignificant
actions of someone else. Don't allow others
to control the direction of your life. Don't
allow your emotions to overpower your
intelligence.

— Morgan Freeman

One of the wonderful themes that came out of Alco-holics Anonymous literature is this: "Don't let others rent space in your head." To this I would add: Especially those who are hurting so much themselves that they unconsciously wish to bring you down or control you as well.

Too often in families, neighborhoods, work settings, religious groups, and even nations, there are damaged people who inadvertently seek in turn to damage others. The distorted sense is that if I make others feel badly, I will be justified in how terrible I feel. In such cases, the world is divided into "good" and "bad" based on whether the person meets their demands in the way *they* want them to be met.

Years ago, when I asked a senior colleague how he addresses this with psychologically classified "borderline patients," he responded, "I tell them that I know they are hurting and feel in need, but they have to change if they want to enjoy their life, have more mature friends, and be in a position to be generative and compassionate themselves."

When I supervise helpers and healers who feel under stress in dealing with persons suffering from this disorder or one like it, I remind them that humility is a necessity in the resilient clinician. I note to them, "Please remember that in the short run those demanding patients who are unreflective of their own faults and dysfunctional style will 'win.' Their pathology is greater than your health. Hopefully, in the long run, however, by your being helpful, but able to set limits, they will improve."

When this happens in family relationships as well as with friends, acquaintances, and colleagues at work, the same caution is noted. This is not only so compassionate souls can prevent being destroyed themselves but also so their wonderful presence to others is not destroyed by one or two deeply hurting persons who, from fear of health and joy, unconsciously want to destroy the very light that can help them out of darkness.

15

My Soul Is Tired

Dear Lord, my soul is tired.

The pain that is close to me and in the world brings tears to my eyes—not a usual response for me.

I find that people seem to encourage division and lies rather than a welcoming spirit and the Truth, and I wonder how I have contributed to this.

When I feel helpless, this makes me wonder how I have closed my eyes to the anger, hate, lack of understanding, and unconditional love that has always been there in the world and…in me.

As I think of my own impermanence and eventual death, as I have been taught to do so in spiritual literature and in Sacred Scripture, will I experience faith and wonder at what is next and gratitude for my time here, or simply fear and doubt about my whole life?

Then I see the little and systemic problems that prey on so, so many and think, Where are You, Lord, amid it all?

Finally, in a quiet moment, when I feel You sitting at my side, I smile, feel secure, and look ahead, not only to what I can do and be for others but to appreciate how in so many ways you are here now and will always be for me in so many ways.

I am at peace.

16

What Is Your Destiny
... Your "Calling"?

If you want to build a ship, don't drum up the
men to gather wood, divide the work, and
give orders. Instead, teach them to yearn for
the vast and endless sea.

— Antoine de Saint-Exupéry

In the delightful and instructive book *Bones of the Master*, the author George Crane at one point shares a story about a Chan (Chinese Buddhist) Master who was planning to return to China to rebuild his temple. He had left there during the Cultural Revolution at a time when monks were killed and temple grounds were destroyed. As part of his efforts he was going to bring a large and heavy marble statue of the Buddha back into the country.

In response to this plan, Crane asked him, "Are you sure? Won't the Government just tear it down?" to which the Master responded, "Not my problem, Georgie. My karma is to rebuild my temple. If they tear it down, that is their karma."

Karma is a Sanskrit term that literally means "action" or "doing." In the Buddhist tradition, karma refers to action driven by intention that leads to future consequences. In other religious traditions, this refers to the importance of living a compassionate life.

This interaction came to mind when I decided to make a positive gesture to a fellow who wasn't very nice to me. Someone familiar with what had happened said to me when she heard about what I was doing, "It will be interesting to see his reaction." To which I replied, "My karma is to send this along. However he reacts is his karma."

Too often we take actions based on whether they are expected to be effective or not. Yet, while success is fun, it is not a determinant of our destiny or, if you will, our karma. Moreover, there are many times when you don't really know what impact your actions are having on someone.

After completing a master of arts degree in clinical psychology at St. John's University in New York, I entered the doctoral program at Hahnemann Medical College in Philadelphia. It was a fairly intense program. Within three years, I had taken forty-four courses and completed three internships. The internships were three days a week, ten months per year. The other two days during the week were spent in class.

One of my internships was at Hahnemann Hospital in its psychiatric unit. When I would come into the building to go up to the seventeenth floor, I would encounter an elderly, curt elevator operator. She would never smile, nor would she involve herself in discussion of any kind. For some reason though, I decided that each morning I was there, I would smile and warmly greet her. She never responded. I never stopped.

When I was finishing the internship, I mentioned as I was leaving that it would be my last day. Much to my surprise, her face lit up and she said she would miss me and my cheery disposition.

Our destiny, calling, or karma is not made up primarily of large or dramatic actions. Instead, it is a lifetime of small intentional steps—some of which would be seen as foolish if taken only from the vantage point of the recipient or onlooker. Yet, our destiny is determined by what we do each day and prompts us to ask ourselves in the evening simple questions to learn about how we lived out our destiny that day.

These are some questions to ask with a sense of intrigue rather than self-blame or projection onto others:

- Did I offer people the "psychological and spiritual space" to rest their burdens, share their joys, and feel secure enough to note their discouragement, anger, sarcasm, sense of alienation, doubts, and fears?
- Was I able to greet others with a smile and help them enjoy a few moments because I listened to them with real interest rather than simply remaining quiet while waiting for an opportunity to speak?
- Did I let go of my own ego, resentments,

and needs long enough for others to share
their own story?
- Was I able to offer some peace and clarity
  and a way for others to be more resilient
  by how I treated them and by what I said?

If someone would ask me if I have done any good
in this world, my response would be, "I hope so, but I
think mostly in ways I didn't expect and about which
I will never know." However, at the very least, even
though I have failed again and again and continue to
do so, in asking myself questions like the ones above, I
feel that I keep trying...no matter what the outcome is.

17

Small Points of Light in the Darkness

One of the joys in my life has been mentoring professionals in the fields of mental health, medicine, nursing, ministry, education, and social work. They are so attuned to themselves that they easily do much of the work on their own.

Recently, a psychologist came in to see me. When he sat down, the expression on his face was one of wistfulness, yet there was also a spark of hope in his eyes. Not knowing how to interpret this, I asked, "How are you doing? You have a look on your face I can't seem to fully fathom, but I sense something significant has happened to you recently."

In response, he laughed and said, "You certainly have spotted my mixed feelings at this point, so let me explain."

He then went on to say he had been feeling overwhelmed for a number of personal and professional reasons. First, he said, his son was sick, and he was feeling helpless about it. Then, the COVID-19 pandemic had not only caused disruption for his patients but also for him. Finally, the horrible things coming out of persons' mouths after the presidential election of 2020 had also disheartened him. He said, "I was honestly worried that I would be brought down by the combination of these things, as well as by other events that were disruptive." Knowing his generous spirit, I was not surprised when he also added, "This made me worry that I wouldn't be able to be as compassionate and professionally astute as I needed to be when facing the issues others who are in such pain brought to me."

Given the mixed message I thought I picked up originally, I asked, "Do you still feel in that space at this point or has something changed?"

He laughed again, and said, "Something *has* changed, and it was the silliest thing that brought me a sense of perspective and peace. I decided I needed to take a walk. I have found that when I get fresh air and a little exercise walking in my neighborhood it usually makes me feel better. You know, the oxygen exchange. When I did this, I passed across the street two women from the neighborhood. They smiled at me and we exchanged brief greetings. Then after we moved on a few steps in opposite directions, I felt a positive impulse, turned, and said to them, 'I always feel better when I meet the two of you taking a nice walk.' They smiled in return and thanked me for my kind words.

"As I walked on further, I felt better. It was like they were points of light in the darkness. I took in their warmth and gratefulness. In addition, the insight came to me that I could only help whoever is in front of me. I couldn't fix the whole world—even the whole of *my* world and the suffering it contained. While it didn't change all I was facing, somehow I felt a sense of refreshing peace."

What this psychologist was appreciating anew is that regaining a healthy perspective need not require major events. When we are "in the now" and open to what crosses our path, small points of light can pierce our darkness. Paradoxically, we can be restored by recognizing not only our gifts but their limits. Such limits need not depress us. They can actually be reminders of our own humanity in a way that we can continue to be compassionate even when we don't achieve immediate positive results, as desirable as they may be. Instead, at such moments, the window to appreciating the "small" gifts in our lives and the willingness to sit with others in the darkness without an end in sight can occur. As a little girl said when asked how she helped a friend in trouble, "I just sat down next to her and helped her cry."

On your own cloudy days, I hope your perspective is opened wide enough to see the points of light in the darkness. I think you will be positively surprised when they show up in such initially small ways but eventually can have a surprisingly significant impact.

18

Two Surprising, Strange Spiritual Experiences

Years ago I remember being in a particularly discouraging situation. In that period, during one of the regular times I spent in silence and solitude with God, a couple of surprising events occurred. First, a piece of Scripture rose to the surface that I had read again and again but never truly appreciated until then. The words were, "They did terrible things to me and the prophets before me. They will do the same to you and worse at times." Following this, what I sensed God saying to me was, "Bob, normally you say religious or spiritual words, and people smile and embrace you, but when things get difficult, you want to run away." All true.

I once had a similar experience in the middle of the night (early morning really). While I thought of the enormous number of people who would vote for someone who had no integrity and had a dangerous personality disorder that had already hurt so many, it woke me from a doze to being wide awake. Then, out of the blue I thought of Jesus on the cross and Mary, his mother, and John, the disciple whom he loved, at the foot of the cross. I saw in my mind's eye that as they looked up at him their sadness was great. As I joined them by imaging him in my mind, I could see he wasn't being crucified alone now: women who had been verbally, sexually, and physically abused were with him on the cross; children who were strangers and fearful being away from home were with him being crucified; strangers who asked for welcome but were turned away were with him in pain; and persons who were choking on impure air and polluted water were dying with him as well.

Also, in envisioning Mary and John at the foot of the cross, feeling Jesus's pain, in feeling helpless as I did, I could identify with them more now than ever as I encountered people in my life who were ill and suffering. On top of this, in my role as a "resiliency psychologist" in seeking to reach out to other helping and healing professionals who were trying to care for others while worrying about their own family and health, I could see how people were able to achieve a healthier sense of perspective when they faced the actual, specific, suffering of others.

Well, as you can imagine, I was totally awake after this and, while I was incredulous at why God would allow this suffering, I was also brought back to my time among the suffering in Calcutta when I recalled the words of Jack Nelson. He also had been there and noted, "While walking the streets of Calcutta, when I saw the suffering of the poor, I began to scream at God. Then I realized that in the suffering of the poor, God was screaming at me."

In reflecting on the "Saints of Germany" who

risked their lives hiding and saving Jewish people during the Nazi era, someone said, "I don't want to be among those who said, 'I didn't know.' I want to do something about the way our country is going. But what can I do? How can I care for those suffering? How can religious persons behave this way?"

My response was quite practical because I find that knee-jerk reactions can simply add hurt and not help situations. I said,

> *First*, do nothing other than ventilate your sense of sorrow, frustration, anger, and incredulity at those who would vote for someone with so little, if any, integrity and how returning him and his colleagues to power is going to cause so much suffering—while the persons voting this way think and shout they are proclaiming gospel values.

> *Second*, when you feel more at peace, or at least steadier, think of individuals—actual persons you know—who are suffering so you can put things in perspective, as Mother Teresa did as she lifted people in the streets, one by one. This will help you feel less overwhelmed by the bigger picture and closer to being able to accomplish something that you can actually do.

Third, continue to pray, because when you do so, it connects your limited efforts to meet God with other people praying in their limited way and with the unlimited power of God that demonstrates itself in sometimes invisible and strange ways. In doing this, you will eventually find that, rather than losing your faith, you are relying less on a religious structure that people make the mistake of worshiping instead of using it as a wonderful bridge to a dynamic God that has been passed down to us. You may actually find in your helplessness that in centering on God's will and doing simply (not "just") what you can, your faith will deepen and mature.

Finally, recognize that being a healing presence to others may be difficult, but despair is unnecessary, and doing what you can while letting other good people and God take care of the residue is honorable and a gate to helpful humility. Having low expectations and high hopes is not only psychologically better...it is the music of prayer.

19

The One Word We
Need to Remember
in Tough Times

Long before psychology and psychiatry embraced the essential value of having the right perspective, religion emphasized it. Wisdom figures teach us that in the Talmud we do not see things as they are...we see things as *we* are. In the Christian New Testament, Matthew 6:22 says, "If your eye is good, your whole body will be good." Buddhists speak about it as the "unobstructed vision" and Hindus in the Upanishads as a "turning around in one's seat of consciousness." We even sense it behind comments of religious teachers through the ages. For instance, the prophet Muhammed is purported to have said at one point, "If you have enough money to buy two loaves of bread, buy only one...and spend the rest on flowers."

A healthy perspective does a number of things to help us avoid unnecessary suffering and to embrace the joy and support around us. In other words, it is a portal to resilience. It does this by alerting us to pick up our emotions so we can stop, reflect, and review our thinking, which can become distorted in a crisis. One example of such distortions is evident when people react in extremes. Some see crises occurring and panic, others fall into a sense of minimization and denial, while still others begin projecting the blame onto some thing or person outside themselves.

Another temptation is to fall back into the silver casket of nostalgia or to project into the future without doing anything in the present. On the other hand, a sense of prayerfulness (being in the present with your eyes wide open to seeing what God may be teaching us *now*) is a key to a healthy perspective.

A healthy perspective also doesn't deny the tough times in life. Instead, it faces them directly with the understanding that it is not the amount of darkness in the world or even in ourselves that matters. It is how we stand in that darkness that is crucial. And so, it is worth the effort to enhance a healthy perspective by taking a few simple but significant steps.

> *First*, anytime you have a powerful emotion (either negative or positive for that matter), ask yourself what you were thinking and believing that produced such a reaction. What often passes for common sense is actually common nonsense that has not been recognized or challenged.

> *Second*, see what is within your control, and what isn't, so you can expend your energy on the right things, because the self is limited.

Third, while not denying negative events in life or playing them down through psychological or spiritual romanticism, be open to how the situation can call you to become deeper as a person. This is known broadly in the psychological literature as "posttraumatic growth" and in theological works as the "spirituality of suffering." A simple example is that in being open to the possible new wisdom you may gain during a crisis or tragedy, you may also find that you are now more in tune with the fragility of life and therefore stop rushing to your grave while thinking you will live forever. The increased silence and solitude of being at home for greater lengths of time because of illness or the lockdown of a pandemic, for example, may also give you the space to enjoy being with yourself more, increase appreciation for the friends you have, and make you value the need to reflect on what is truly important in life—instead of what society is trying to convince you is.

Crises are horrible and, of course, shouldn't be welcomed or made light of. Make no mistake about this. However, when they do occur, *the darkness they bring need not be the last word.* Instead, paradoxically, such times may actually offer the first step in seeing and living life in positive ways that would not have been possible had they not happened in the first place. Opening your eyes to this positive potential won't make the tragedy any less but it will increase the chance you won't miss its hidden possibilities going forward. And this is essential to grasp given the negative events all of us must go through at different times in life.

20

Relieving the Anxiety
...Focusing on the Ultimate

One of my favorite Orthodox Christian spirituality writers is Kyriacos Markides, who is the author of *Gifts of the Desert* and *The Mountain of Silence*.

In one of his books he speaks about a friend on the island of Cyprus sharing with him an experience he had just prior to having surgery. He said he was very anxious about having the procedure until he spoke to a priest he respected.

When Markides asked what the priest said that put him at ease, the man said, "Father told me not to wish for anything other than God's will taking place—whatever the outcome might be." He said that after hearing this and praying that way, immediately his anxiety left him, and he felt free.

That story came back to me when I thought about an upcoming presidential election. Whatever would happen, although I would do everything in my power to make the right choice and encourage others to take everything into account before making theirs, my primary hope and what I focused on in prayer was that God's will would be done.

I plan to remember this going forward in other areas of my life as well. It follows the old Ignatian theme of acting as if everything is in my hands while knowing, in the end, it is all in God's. There is deep peace in this for me...maybe for you as well.

21

Being Open to "The Next Step"

A while back I remember giving a copy of an edited work I had published to a recently ordained priest whom I had just met. A week or so later he sent me a nice letter of thanks for the gift. However, it initially had a surprisingly negative impact on me because of how the letter was addressed and signed. Even though I am three times his age, have been a professor in universities and seminaries, and a therapist and mentor to clergy and religious, he addressed it, "Dear Robert" and signed it, "Rev. _____."

In response, I was annoyed and thought, "Well, isn't that immature!…Why don't seminaries teach persons on their road to priesthood to be more respectful toward those older than they are?…Don't they read Scripture where it is written that Jesus didn't cling to his divinity?" I was on a roll in prayer. Then a strange thing happened during my usual morning quiet time after that. I sensed Jesus ask me to be open to taking "the next step" in *my own* life.

What I felt God was asking me at that moment

was, "Why are you upset over this man's behavior? If you are made in my image and likeness and I have your name carved in the palm of my hand, isn't that the only identity that really matters? Did I not also say, in your favorite Gospel, 'I have called you friend'? (John 15:15). Moreover, instead of wasting energy on protecting your unnecessarily inflated image, shouldn't you be sharing that very vitality with people who are poor, physically ill, and experiencing psychological distress who *really* need your compassion?"

Such questions helped me take the next step. I realized that noticing what people do, and positing the possible reason for any unhelpful behavior on their part, may be natural in today's society. No problem. However, spending undue energy on it often means I have forgotten the scriptural lessons before me that should be in my heart to lead me deeper in my relationship with God and to live a richer life for others.

Still, it is easier to embrace such graces if we take time each day in silence and solitude with a sense of openness to learn about ourselves and personalize God's teachings further. We also need such daily space to enjoy God's visits rather than miss them.

In addition, it is helpful to possess in prayer an attitude marked by *intrigue* rather than defensiveness, self-blame, and discouragement. The motivation in true prayer is to go deeper in our relationship with God in a way that the *fruit of freedom* from unnecessary worries, anger, disappointment, defensiveness, doubt, narcissism, and stress can be both seen and embraced by us. It is called "the spiritual life."

22

Feeling Defeated and Discouraged?

Possibly a Sign of Something New

As the morning breaks over the water behind my house, it reminds me of new hope. When I ask some people why they are consulting me, they reply that they feel defeated and discouraged. After chatting with them for a while, one of my goals is to help them realize that rather than simply something negative, such emotions are often signs that they are turning a corner in life.

As a young driver learns, making a turn is harder than simply going straight ahead. In turning you are moving from what you can easily see to a place that is new and temporarily hidden, and which often holds a radically different view of life…*your* life.

The temptation is to avoid necessary turns and to simply seek to go where you can see, what you are used to. But the discouragement and feelings of defeat, especially as we move from one stage in life to another, are calls to let go of the past, not preoccupy yourself with places you may never go, and be in the present in a new way.

Change cannot be avoided—whether seen initially as desirable or horrible. The key is how we meet necessary change and whether we will allow it to soften our soul and open us up or simply have us pull over, park our life, and refuse to make the psychological and spiritual turns we are being called to make…for our own sake and those who count on us.

By the way, it is all right to park for a while. But my hope is that you will eventually have the courage to pull out into the "traffic" again and make the turns necessary for you at times. You will be much happier and experience more of life in the end.

23

Reading Between the Lines and Looking Further …A Portal to Spiritual Self-Awareness

When receiving and offering spiritual mentoring, many topics come up. In such instances, sometimes there is a disagreement on the views taken between the mentor and person seeking guidance. In such cases, a turning point is reached when the topic itself takes a minor place in the discussion. At that juncture, what can be learned about the person being mentored, who happens to be holding a particular position, becomes more important. The question is whether the person being guided will be able to pick up the unspoken theme that is "between the lines."

This has come back to me again and again when I have posted something online. When I get a longer than usual response that is filled with intensity, I try to follow up if I feel called to do so. My hope is that they will psychologically and spiritually "lean back" and reflect further, not simply on the issue at hand but by reading between the lines of the pros and cons of the discussion. I want them to look further at *why* they have responded with such energy, *at this time*, *in this way*, and what they can learn about *themselves* that will enable greater spiritual self-knowledge. The first responses they have are often not helpful, but if they are willing to look further, there is much for them to learn about themselves.

Yet, I often get responses like the following: "I am sorry, but this is how I feel." "You are not going to change my mind." "We feel differently about what is truly important." "I think you are being fooled."

Now, while such statements may be accurate, they are truly not the point and close the portal to greater spiritual self-knowledge for them, which is sad.

You might then ask, "Why do you continue to follow up with them?" My response is simple and twofold: (1) The unconscious defensive reaction they have, rather than being willing to look further into themselves, reminds me that I do the same at times and so puts me on greater guard against my own blocks to growth and change. In dealing with their defensiveness, I am encouraged by their resistance to look further at mine and to pray for the grace to open up my personality to further transformation. And (2) The second reason is simple: My calling is to gently nudge others to psychologically and spiritually lean back from their views, reactions, and intensity to look further at their own motivations, fears, and needs. I also don't want them to miss the wonder and possibilities within themselves that lie just beneath their negative feelings.

The excuse that one feels strongly about something is usually a psychological cloak that covers and prevents humility, new insight, and openness to growth. As one guide said to *me* when I defended myself by saying I was sorry but this is how I felt: "Please remember, Jesus only got crucified once. Look at your many motivations and know that emotions often indicate the need for greater humility, not an indication that your strongly held views are totally correct." I really do need to get more gentle mentors in my life.

24

When
...Moving from an Initial Negative Impulse to a Positive Response

In challenging times we are surrounded by negative stimuli. Those who truly care and are sensitive, rather than being those who yell the loudest when they know the least, are in an unusual position. On the one hand, they are most vulnerable to becoming discouraged, burned out, and overwhelmed. On the other hand, with a sense of openness and a desire to go deeper into themselves, they have an increased possibility of experiencing growth, a healthier perspective, and greater inner strength than they had before. There are simple steps all of us can take *when* confronted by darkness (we will be). After reading the responses to a few scenarios, I suggest you come up with several more you expect would be helpful in your effort to not only survive but actually thrive in new ways. Just to start you off:

When the news primarily highlights U.S. Congress members fighting among themselves and the leaders playing golf, while the suffering of others is surging, one's immediate reaction may be anger. But this is also a call to pray for them since, like all of us, they will eventually meet God and have to answer the question, How have you increased love in this world by what you said and did? As the saying goes: "At the end of the game, the queen and the pawn go into the same box."

When we hear the voices of older Christians lamenting in these times, "When will young people return to church?" we must remember many never were part of it, and that is not bad. When young people see prominent adults around them worshiping idols and rules rather than the living God, who wants us to be welcoming to and caring of those different from us, we need to recognize it is good that young people refuse to join in such hypocrisy. And so, they have a chance to come anew to the beauty of Christianity in a courageous way and build a bridge to God where they can pray, love Scripture anew, and form a community of love that taps into the tradition bequeathed to us by Jesus.

When we find ourselves wanting to stay current on events and find ourselves being dragged down each morning as we watch or read the news, we will know that our desire is a good one. Yet, we will limit it to only five minutes of headlines, rather than be pulled into the swamp of negativity by hearing the same terrible news covered from five different angles. In embracing the dark side of life during the few moments we receive a necessary awareness of what is going on, we can then also use such stimuli to move in the other direction.

We can search for and recall all the good that is also going on in this world that we wouldn't have seen had the tragedy not spurred on such a response by many in the first place.

When neighbors, coworkers, family, and friends seem to focus primarily on the negative when they meet us, this can also be a signal to find those in our social circle who are positive, healing, have a sense of humor, and are involved in positive activities and insights not possible had the challenging times not dawned in the first place.

Yes, there are challenges we didn't have before that won't go away soon. There are, however, responses that can surprisingly not only lift us up but also make us stronger than we have ever been *when* we respond in a healing, helping, discerning way that releases us from the coffin of nostalgia, helps us put down the menu of fantasy about the future, and has us enjoy with more relish what we have in our life now, because we are grateful for what we used to take for granted.

(And, if none of the above works, have a good rest tonight and know you will be more renewed in the morning!)

25

Don't You Believe It

Once I heard a story about a sage who was tired of hearing unbridled praise for certain hermits that others admired for their constant poise and serenity. Having finally heard enough, he said, "Just bring them down from the mountain, give them a spouse and some children, let them get a job, pay taxes, and face an illness in the family, and we'll see how quickly they lose their aura…and patience!"

Having treated, mentored, and supervised psychiatrists, psychologists, counselors, social workers, physicians, nurses, physician assistants, military leaders, and persons in full-time ministry, I would concur. The image we have of those who are helpers and healers is neither realistic nor fair to them…or to yourself, for that matter.

It is not fair to them because it puts them on a pedestal and, in the process, prevents them from recognizing it is perfectly natural for them to feel poorly at times. It is understandable when they temporarily feel sorry for themselves and silently scream to themselves that answering the call to be a caregiver doesn't give others the license to make them into martyrs. We saw this in the case of those during the COVID-19 pandemic who refused to wear masks and didn't take precautions to avoid crowded bars and packed parties. The result? They sometimes wound up becoming infected with the virus, and because of their arrogance and ignorance, wound up overwhelming ICU hospital wards as well as nurses and other helpers who were tasked with helping them.

Rather than believing that "if *only* I could be more like this special person, guru, therapist, priest, or other type guide, I would be stronger and not feel poorly," which causes you to think you are not enough, recognize that all people feel that way at times. Emotional sadness, feeling a bit confused by it all, finding yourself worrying and going around in circles—this happens to all of us, whether or not we are helpers and leaders. Instead, it is helpful to view such disruptive periods in life as ideal "knocks on your psychological and spiritual doors" to further open your mind and heart to reflection and the need to rest and renew in creative, even small, ways. They are also calls for something more basic: a simple suggestion on how to maintain a healthy perspective when feeling lost.

Such a perspective is seen in the words of Thomas Merton that I love and often share with others. He once said to an older monk who was feeling "down" and fearful of losing his faith, "Courage comes and goes....Hold on for the next supply!"

Patience, perseverance, and, yes, even courage are necessary as your emotions move up and down at times. Eventually, your mood will change. Moreover, if you keep aware of what all of it is teaching you, much can be learned. The simple gifts and persons around you will be appreciated more. Also, of equal importance, you will be in a position to support others when they need it most. When you have respected and embraced your own vulnerability, you can teach them to do so as well because you have been there...you have been kind to and understanding of your emotions...you have learned from the dysfunctional thoughts and beliefs that caused them...and, most important, you have learned that humility teaches us to hold on for the next supply of courage.

26

Wake Up Stories
for Us...*Now*

Life-giving stories continually wake up my unconsciously imprisoned spirit *if* I remain open enough
to let their lessons teach me. In my work with helpers
and healers from such countries as Haiti, Rwanda, and
Syria, I have always found my interactions with those
I serve to be a "circle of grace" for me. Although I am
technically in the role of "mentor," the stories I hear
often express the most illuminating examples of true
compassion and unbelievable resilience in leading a rich
life—no matter what might be going on for them in
their own country or life at the time.

Among the twenty countries where I have presented material on self-care, resilience, maintaining a
healthy perspective, and integrating psychology with
classic spirituality, many were in Asia. Stories that I
heard firsthand from persons in Vietnam, Cambodia,
the Philippines, China, Japan, and Thailand often held
cultural surprises that made it easier for me to unlearn,
let go, and view myself and my style of thinking in new

and revealing ways. Recently, a story told by a Tibetan reminded me of this.

He was asked what he feared most when he was being held, demeaned, and tortured in a Chinese prison. His answer? Not what I thought—and certainly *not* the answer I might have given if I were in a similar situation! He said, "I was worried I would lose my compassion for those who were treating me this way."

During one American presidential election, I didn't believe I should have had to worry as this Tibetan did… but I should have! I fooled myself by taking the just causes of people on the margins (poor, ill, demeaned, downtrodden) and the desire to build a community of kindness and combined my concern about them with my own ego and anger. There is such a thing as "justified anger" at injustices and actions motivated by narcissism, greed, fear, and others' desire for revenge. Yet, as I watched such persons even use the Bible and religion to excuse and justify terrible actions, in the process, I failed to watch *myself* as well.

When we lose deep compassion for *everyone*, we corrupt this virtue and beautiful signature strength. When we don't see the dangers caused by poor motivations for our actions—even in support of the most noble causes—we can contaminate them with our own willfulness. We also prevent what dramatic challenges can teach us, and remind us of, that is essential.

As a Chan Master, Tsung Tsai, when questioned about the pillars of life, responded, "Compassion. Just compassion…and strength." A friend who knew Tsung Tsai well reflected about him and what he had faced early in life by noting, "At home that night I thought of all he had endured [as a monk during the Chinese Cultural Revolution]. It had stripped him of all that was false" (George Crane, *Bones of the Master*).

With these two stories in mind, in recent days I have revisited and reflected again on the days leading up to and immediately following the U.S. presidential election of 2020. As I thought about the Tibetan prisoner who feared losing compassion for his captors and the Chan Master who went through such terrible times as a Buddhist in Communist China, I asked myself, "What caused me during the election period to fail to keep compassion in my heart and sadness for the world before my eyes?" Certainly, I didn't want to add to the horrible and divisive actions and words of others with my own uncaring actions and words. Why didn't I stand up for others with a *purer heart* so I wouldn't say or do things simply to release my anger and frustration, cover my feelings of helplessness, and unnecessarily negatively add to the situation?

With clarity and kindness gained through taking out time in silence and solitude to be mindful, I didn't have to feel helpless, hopeless, angry, and fearful. Instead, in those quiet moments, as well as through helpful reading and interaction with friends wiser than I was, I could welcome a greater understanding of how and why I was thinking as I did about the events around me. I could face injustice with a true spirit of caring and resilience rather than expressing "shotgun anger" or defeatism. I could draw on the strength of community while embracing anew the Cameroonian proverb: "If you want to go fast, go alone…If you want to go far, go together."

However, I could only do this if I were able to see the impurity in my motives. Whereas, if I were able to see the primacy of compassion for everyone, I could be stronger for others and within myself in ways that would improve the situation rather than make it worse.

Yes, the Chan Master was correct: "Compassion. Just compassion…and strength."

27

Two Amazing Journeys!

There are so many challenging things going on around us. Yet, during very external events such as these, the most amazing journeys involve attending not to what is around us as much as to what is *within* us. As a matter of fact, how we avoid or enter into our attitudes during such dramatic, enduring events will ultimately determine the fate of how we live our lives going forward.

Two journeys within that get attenuated—especially at junctures when the world around us is in a flurry—are ones involving how we look at our own growing edges and gifts. Such formative efforts on our part can make a heaven out of an apparent hell and vice versa.

Long ago, I had very good fortune come within my grasp. Since I am a proud person, it turned out to be an even greater treasure. What happened was that I realized that every negative comment made about me, no matter how poor the motivation of the person saying it, was true to some extent. And if I had the wherewithal not to become defensive or beat myself up because of what hurtful remarks were made, I would become freer than I ever was before. I could mine such truths for what value and accuracy they held and, rather than either getting angry or despairing of who I was as a human being, seize an ideal chance to learn and grow while also being loosened from the opinions of others.

The other journey within that struck me as so beneficial was when I was praised for psychological gifts I had been given—and I say *gifts* because they were present almost from birth, so I couldn't take credit for their presence. The first part of the journey was to recognize them and feed them fully so they would not only be a joy to me but also a means to be present and compassionate in ways that others with different gifts could not.

This second journey within did not end there. I finally saw that I had lesser "signature strengths" or virtues that I hadn't given as much psychological or spiritual air to breathe. As an adult, it remains fun looking for them within and sharing them freely with others, expecting nothing in return. I felt like a hidden Santa Claus traveling year-round. Then I noticed something totally surprising: in uncovering and expressing the quiet personality gifts I had been given in life, without my knowing it, they were also pruning and deepening the major gifts that had marked earlier years in my life:

- Passion was now often tempered and enriched by gentleness
- Humor became more joyful for others when I took greater care in its expression
- Knowledge grew into wisdom when I would allow humility to deflate my ego

- Helpful comments to others were received more readily when delivered in a kinder, more timely fashion

The list could go on for all of us, and the best part is that it has almost nothing to do with us! It is pure grace. The work is almost done by itself when we have the right attitude marked by openness, attentiveness, and a willingness to learn about ourselves for our whole lives. Isn't that wonderful?

And so, while the news we watch, read, and exchange with each other, at times, seems so loud and defining of our lives, there is some quiet new information that is even more important now. This "good news" comes from within and can determine our *lasting* levels of peace and joy in ways that no news from without can ever do...because everything changes at some point. Birth leads to death for everyone. Gatherings lead eventually to dispersion. Possessions gained are eventually lost. Experiences that are positive will fade in time. Our attitude, however, remains with us for our whole life. Since we are with ourselves more than with anyone else, the journeys within to visit our attitude and keep it fresh with new knowledge and healthier through a sense of mindfulness about each moment are more crucial than visits to the television, internet, cell phone, or even a friend's house.

And the nice thing is this: we can begin this journey at any time in our lives and know it will have an instant good return on our time investment. All journeys that have us looking in the wrong direction can change and have us turn around and look in a more helpful one. Therefore, let's join together in letting go of blaming others and events, attacking ourselves, or becoming discouraged; instead, let's welcome a sense of intrigue about who we are and how we can enjoy and share what we have learned about ourselves by being more compassionate to those around us.

28

"Psychological Contagion"

When I was in Beirut, I was asked to speak to physicians, relief workers, and other caregivers who were working in Aleppo, Syria, and had come to Lebanon for a break and to hear me speak on resilience, self-care, and maintaining a healthy perspective. After a few moments of interacting with them, I could see they were quite burned out. Some were also angry at the world that would allow such terror, torture, bombings, and unnecessary illness to occur. In working with them, I knew that if I were to remain strong enough to provide what help I could, I would need to psychologically lean back from their darkness so I could offer what light (healthier perspective) that I could. They certainly deserved anything I could do for them. In the process, I knew it would also be natural for some to project anger and helplessness onto me since they felt safe enough to do so. Without allowing myself some psychological distance to understand their actions, I would be pulled down, unnecessarily personalize their comments, and not be of service to anyone.

Such a dramatic encounter brought me back to a time when I was a student for my doctorate in psychology at Hahnemann Medical College and Hospital. The interaction I recalled was a much less intense interaction with a neighbor but still one that was psychologically crushing for her. She felt that she was on the edge of a divorce and had come to visit with my wife and me to ventilate her worries, feel the freedom to cry in front of other human beings, and share her burden.

After she left, my wife said to me, "You didn't seem upset by what she was saying." And, to this, I responded, "Oh, I was but didn't feel I had the liberty to let myself feel it while she was here because I needed to remain clear so I could offer her what clarity and emotional support I could. I knew she came partially because of the clinical work I did and the studies I was involved in at the time."

I was to think of this later when one of my patients said to me, "I notice that you laugh with me, but you never cry in my presence." She then quickly added, "But then I thought to myself: 'Yes, he does cry, but in his own time when he is by himself.'"

These stories contain two important realities for me. The first one is that psychological stress cannot only hurt us but also our ability to reach out to others who really need our support at certain moments. Second, all of us need to give ourselves time to grieve not only the loss of a family member or friend but also a world that has become so divisive, self-centered, narcissistic, and harsh.

And so, we need to be aware when we are being emotionally pulled in and down by those we meet— not so we can tell them this or become resentful that they would put this on us, but so we can be a good listener and an encouraging voice as we would want close friends and colleagues to be for us at times. In addition, we need to recognize the electronic messengers—television and the internet—as well as printed news sources that endanger us. Only negative news is presented as important; even when a television show tries to present positive stories, it is often at the end of the show and therefore not placed with a sense of prominence.

Finally, we do need time to mourn, either by ourselves or with someone whose presence will not exacerbate the negative but will allow a space for us to let go of what is dark, in order to make room for what is light.

Crescendos of negative news, or when they are prolonged in our life more than we had expected, need to be recognized, understood, and trimmed so they aren't given a chance to set up tents within us. This is not tantamount to denial and "spiritual or psychological romanticism"; it is simple common sense. Staying psychologically afloat takes careful thinking, dealing with what you can handle so as to make some impact, and having an eye to what the darkness, maybe *especially* the darkness, has to teach us, so we can live life as fully and as compassionately as possible going forward.

29

Seasons of Joy for Others ...Peace for Us Within

In general, and especially when we enter more deeply into the season of Advent and look ahead to Christmas, the timing is right to be called to be less self-absorbed and more generative in ways in which we give of ourselves...expecting nothing in return. True *mitzvah*.

Years ago, when one of my closest friends was very sick, we were chatting over the phone and he said he was worried. I asked him what it was that was causing upset. He replied, "With this cancer, I hope I don't lose my ability to read. I love to read." He eventually did lose clear enough eyesight so he couldn't read easily.

Later on during a visit with him, he raised another fear. I asked, "What is it that you are afraid of now?" He said, "They are now talking about hospice. I have some fear of dying." And we discussed it.

Finally, on a visit where the two of us were alone, he admitted to another fear, and I thought to myself, what could he possibly be afraid of after all he shared? He said, "I am afraid that I will no longer be able to be compassionate."

As all of us enter further into the spiritual seasons of our life, when crises shine a brighter light on our needs, fears, sense of separation from others, and personal discomforts, let us follow the lead of my dear friend who died and allow these blessed seasons to soften our souls, open our hearts more deeply, and appreciate the "circle of grace" that is the true compassion we have for others—a reminder of the greater love God has for us.

30

My Father Never Took
a Walk with Me

As a therapist, now that I am later in life, my work involves giving presentations on self-care, resilience, and maintaining a healthy perspective. It also includes mentoring professional helpers and healers. In their case, it isn't psychotherapy since we are not focusing on problems or issues they are facing. Instead, it is about them turning a new, necessary corner in their lives. With only a little nudge or question, they usually do all the work on self-discovery and challenge themselves to move deeper in their lives and the work they are called to do as compassionate guides to others. As one colleague said about such mentoring, "It is like watching a fish fileting itself."

In one such mentoring session, a fairly well-known professional guide and writer, then in his forties, shared with me that his father never took a walk with him. Surprised, and sensing this had special meaning for him, I asked, "Well, where does that leave you now?"

He responded, "Well, of course I knew this all my adult life after he died and that to me it meant a lack of personal connection. However, eventually I realized that it was even more important for me going forward. I saw that as a therapist myself I could react in a number of ways to it that would not only form me but also impact those with whom I lived and those I helped."

"What were the future psychological and spiritual roads you could take?" I asked.

"Well, I could let it define me and so I would always feel needy and believe that people should take care of *me* since I had gone through this in early life. That I needn't put myself out for others because I was the one who had been hurt early on.

"The second choice was more focused on remediating it. I could make a special effort not to treat my own children like I was treated.

"However, there was a more profound calling I felt from what had happened to me as a child. It was to be grateful to all the people now who, and events which, I have in my life that others didn't and to accept those who, unlike me, weren't able to be grateful as I was. I needed to have low expectations and high hopes for others and stop focusing so much on myself and my sense of entitlement."

All of us in life have had experiences like this man had. The question for us, like him, is whether we want to let those experiences define us for the rest of our lives in a way that is not helpful to us or others, or whether we wish to be open to let such tough times "soften our soul" so we can be even more gracious with others given what we have experienced. Once again, the choice is there for us to make during the brief time we are given on this earth that we call "a lifetime."

31

"Do You Have a Moment?"

As I mentioned in the introduction to this book, after a presentation or when encountering someone who has read my work, it is not unusual for that someone to ask, "Do you have a moment for a question?" Usually, since I have built in time for such individual questions, I am able to respond, "Yes, I do. How may I help you?"

In their responses, one of the common themes that comes up is an existential one. It is also the one most often asked around the start of the new year, and those who ask it are often over fifty. To paraphrase and combine some of what has been asked of me over the past thirty-five years on this subject, the question goes something like this:

> *I am surrounded by family and good friends. Generally I see myself as a happy and fulfilled person. Yet, at times, I have this sense of feeling lost and somehow out of place being who I am. When I feel a bit down because of this vague sense of alienation from even those who love me, I feel ungrateful. Is there something I can do to somehow snap me out of it or to become more*

*grateful for all of the people and possessions I
have present in my life?*

Now, being grateful is of course very important
for psychological and spiritual reasons. Psychologically,
grateful people are the happiest. Not only are they able
to more fully appreciate what is *already* present in their
lives, such an outlook broadens their view of what the
world can offer them going forward. Whereas "entitled
individuals" are tied to what they feel is due to them
in the way they want it delivered, grateful people have
psychological eyes (a healthier perspective), so they
don't take anything for granted. All is gift—including
the chance to take a walk, drink a nice hot cup of tea or
coffee, have an opportunity to be of service in ways that
it is a circle of grace for them, and so many other things
that people who are ungrateful miss.

Yet, the persons asking me about their lack of gratitude are, in reality, often the most grateful persons in
the world. Gratitude is not the issue in their sense of
alienation—an inability to be close to people who really
appreciate their unique spirit is. All of us are quite special, even though we share many traits, interests, and
history with each other. This uniqueness, what persons of faith might refer to as their "name" before God,
needs to be honored for the gift each person can be to
this world.

When I guide such persons in a brief encounter,
I ask them to do two things. First, spend some time
in silence and solitude focusing on Jesus's phrase, "You
are my friend" (John 15:14). During that time seek to

see God smiling on the gifts the Creator has offered that have come to life in us. The second is to ensure you have contact with people who appreciate your gifts and feel they are made better by your presence in their lives—even if they are mere acquaintances or persons interacted with in passing. In doing this, take care not to diminish their positive response to you by saying such things as, "Oh, they are nice to everyone." After all, if you are walking with a friend out onto a beach in Florida on a beautiful clear day, you certainly wouldn't say to your companion, "Oh, let's go inside. This sun is shining on everyone here."

As we become more attuned to God's love for us and reflect God's Spirit, given to us as gift, we have the "eyes" to recognize the gratitude of those whose path we cross. Then we will feel less alienated or alone.

An added benefit of this is that rather than turning our back on our faults because we feel helpless ("Oh, this is just how I am, I guess."), we will view our faults differently. Rather than their being a source of discouragement or self-blame, we will look at them with a sense of intrigue. Because we feel loved and appreciated in concrete ways by God and others, we will become even more interested in pruning the faults we have so the gifts from God that make up our identity will shine even brighter and we will feel less alone and more grateful for the life we are living.

32

A Psychological and Spiritual Winter Solstice

Just as in the case of a physical one, a "psychological and spiritual winter solstice" marks a turning point in time. It doesn't deny enduring a serious period of darkness that is still continuing. Neither does it turn its back on the increasing light to come. Both experiences must be held simultaneously if wisdom, a new way of being, and moving forth with greater appreciation of what is important are possible.

Anyone who romanticizes the darkness is a fool. Also, not to position oneself to benefit from experiences within the darkness and retain hope is equally a mistake. Still, to embark on such a path, we must be willing to embrace our own vulnerability. The cycles of life humble us. When we resist this by hardening our outlook, like rigid branches in the winds of change, something must break in us and also unfortunately fall on those around us in a way that hurts them as well.

Yet, when we are open to the lessons past darkness can teach us and are attuned to the nuances of the ones that remain, they become teachers of what is essential and important in life. Combining clarity and hope can relieve us of old deadening habits and offer a new *horarium*, a "holy routine," for us to entertain.

Pure possibility can be a gift of the cold dark times if we have the eyes to see. In a *New York Times* article, "How We Survive Winter" (December 20, 2020), author Elizabeth Dias quotes Brother Guy Consolmagno, the director of the Vatican Observatory, as saying, "The stars are especially beautiful in the wintertime....Unfortunately, the clearest nights are also the coldest nights, because the clouds act as a blanket to keep the warmth in....It is an interesting metaphysical as well as astronomical truth, that it is only when you have good darkness that you can see the faint lights, whether it is faint stars, or the little points of light, the thousand points of light that bring us hope even in darkness."

The simplicity that is almost forced on us during a lockdown or period of illness can be seen as a chance to view what is important in new ways. Or it can be experienced only as boredom and merely a time to wait for past routines to become possible again. In darkness, the choices we make have us possibly walking through the existential portal to encounter the new light that is only visible during dark times or sinking in a sense of boredom, or simply feeling overwhelmed and dissatisfied, resulting in our missing a rare epiphany (sudden revelation or insight) that is there for the taking...and needed to experience a richer life going forward into the radically new era we will face.

33

A Funny Thing
about Cynicism

A funny thing about cynicism is that it is so popular today. To many people it seems only sensible. Yet, persons who are images of hope today are ones who have gone through terrible, terrible personal ordeals themselves and aren't cynical. Those who feel that hope, joy, and peace are simply exercises in psychological and spiritual romanticism have not fathomed the lives of such persons as the Dalai Lama, Archbishop Desmond Tutu, and other committed good souls who remain filled with joy.

About them, Douglas Abrams, who edited material in *The Book of Joy* on a joint meeting they had, wrote,

> The Dalai Lama and the Archbishop are two of the great spiritual masters of our time, but they are also moral leaders who transcend their own traditions and speak always from a concern for humanity as a whole. Their courage and resilience and dogged hope in humanity inspire millions as they refuse to

give in to the fashionable cynicism that risks engulfing us. Their joy is clearly not easy or superficial but one burnished by the fire of adversity, oppression, and struggle. The Dalai Lama and the Archbishop remind us that joy is in fact our birthright and even more fundamental than happiness.

To reach this point, both leaders are persons who spent time in meditation. They also avoided the dysfunctional thinking that leads to unhelpful emotions and actions. Instead, they took quiet reflective moments—*not* to be with their own ego, contemplate cynical thoughts, or entertain the demands that the world be as they want it to be *now*.

To the contrary, they saw that quiet time, like the stillness of the sea's depths even during a violent storm causing turbulent waves on the surface, allowed them to see clearly, act justly, and remain both compassionate and able to live with a greater sense of meaning.

In seeking to act for good in a troubled world, they knew that the self is limited. And so they sought not to waste energy on what they couldn't control. They did this so they could calmly and clearly focus on what *they* could do to make this a better—and less divisive—world.

Persons of true hope and joy don't play down the darkness around them. Neither do they close the door to hope and stay on the doorstep of new wisdom, complaining about the world, and not entering the next calling of their lives to become humbler, wiser, and more compassionate.

Cynicism? There is not time for this attitude in a world filled with so many good people and so many needs. There just isn't time for it. Don't be fooled. Life is a gift that is very brief for us and those who count on us. Use as role models those who have been through hell but have heaven deep within them. You can be like them. No, it is not too late. Don't use that expensive excuse. Instead, start where you are because that, in reality, is all you can do anyway.

Avoiding the mental immaturity that leads to unbridled anger at the world, self-condemnation, or discouragement, our role models didn't turn their back on injustice. In doing this, they recognized they didn't have the luxury to be sarcastic, filled with self-pity, or give up. They took heart from their quiet times in silence and solitude, wrapped in gratitude. They sought to draw from a community of others who wished the same. And they opened themselves up to learn from those who disagreed and young or "young-at-heart" people, whose purity of heart was not yet contaminated by some adults who felt cynicism equaled reality.

34

When Grace Sneaks Past Our Defenses

One Sunday, a thought occurred to me as I looked around the church. As I scanned the small congregation present, for some reason I could sense my own lies and sins, anger, entitlement, greed, and narcissism. I also thought some of them might have similar sins and failings that, like me, they hide or gloss over, or for which they blame others instead. Yet, I also realized that there were others present who were different. In their simplicity and humility, they were models of compassion for people who are poor and ill and tried to live a life stripped of falsity.

As I pondered all this further, I became grateful for these good "Sunday souls" who were there as a community of prayer to support and encourage me. They were put there, alongside my hearing the Word announced and the Eucharist offered, so I might find my way home to God and my true self.

This grace-filled gift of insight was then followed by another quite surprising one for me. I was sitting in church on a Tuesday morning and suddenly thought to myself, "What am I doing here? It's not Sunday and I only go to church on *Sundays*." The recognition of my being at the earliest Mass on a weekday became even more surprising to me when I realized that I had been going to Mass on Mondays through Thursdays for several months without thinking much about making such a decision. I almost exclaimed out loud in the quiet church to the twenty-five or so people also there, "How did this happen? Who is responsible for this?"

As I brought this awareness to the few moments of silence and solitude that I usually set aside later in the day—which is my normal practice because of the intense work I am sometimes involved in—I realized that a quiet grace of starting most of my days during the week with communal prayer was given to me. I also could see it was a new chance for me to connect with who and what are good that were around and within me.

The church's pastor, who always celebrates the earliest Mass, told me later on he didn't preach at that particular morning service because he wanted it to be a gentle, quiet contemplative Mass. As presider, he also enunciated the words so clearly and slowly that I heard some of the words of the ritual in a surprisingly powerful way—I think maybe for the first time!

All of us are given quiet graces similar to this one to enrich our days and very brief lives. The question is whether our minds will be so filled with our own will, worries, and resistances that there will be no room for such epiphanies or surprises. And, even when someone like myself lives that way, Grace can still sneak up to say something timely and revelatory as to how we are living our lives. Will we listen, reflect, and act to change when it does?

Maybe, even the presence of COVID-19 and the turmoil in the United States and other countries contain such a grace to wake up. In addition, maybe at this point, there is another event you can't explain in your life today that is also a grace waiting for you to see clearer and become more open *now*. Just *maybe*. What do you think? Why not sit and pray with this question for a while before deciding too quickly?

From my own experience, I believe it is too important a possibility to run past in order to live life comfortably as you have done in the past. I truly do.

35

Look at the Needs of the Young…Then Look at Yourself

A Jewish scripture scholar once shared that in the Talmud you do not see things as *they* are; you see things as *you* are. Karl Barth, a Christian theologian, indicated a similar sentiment. He warned that when you read the New Testament and ask, "What is this book saying?" it should respond, "Who is it that is asking?" If you are really reading the Word, your identity is on the line.

The simplest way you can tell when people are in covenant with the Word is by their behavior. Young people avoid religion when they see adults who either have a vague, "simply Sunday" spirituality or they yell scriptural phrases to suit their own needs, defenses, biases, fears, and narcissism. Out of all age groups, young people can recognize the spiritually smug, even if they are wearing a religious garment of some type. Because of this, they may shun becoming involved enough to see the true beauty of a religious tradition that would encourage them to encounter a dynamic God and be part of a compassionate community.

The result of such hypocritical behavior on the part of some adults is also often accompanied by a wistfulness that is misplaced. I remember one woman sighing and sharing with a friend that she wished their new pastor would inspire young people to come back to church. To which her companion made a face and responded, "That's impossible. They were never truly called to be there in the first place."

Wishing for times past not only is useless and destructively ignores the problems hidden back then, but it can also develop into the "sin" of nostalgia because it turns into idol worship of what is dead and not worship of the living God.

On the other hand, when adults are willing to face the complex challenges of all of Scripture, young people

- see efforts to care for people who are poor—and don't merely hear religious words asking God alone to help them;
- observe welcoming strangers—not protecting one's own interests instead;
- appreciate the honesty of admitting one's mistakes and sins—not experiencing the narcissism of defensiveness and "spin";
- understand the power of living in union with God's will (theonomy) as a way to free their own will (autonomy) to seek a rich compassionate and meaningful life;
- become aware of the adventure of the spiritual life in those guiding them at home and in school or a religious setting.

It is true that religious leaders—and I include parents and older siblings, as well as bishops, priests, ministers, and female and male religious ("sisters" and "brothers")—who seek to protect "the church" and sell a religion of security, comfort, self-interest, power, and escapism often are people who know not what they do. Even though this may be so, what they do can leave young people adrift because even though many may feel lost, they don't want to build their life only on a set of rules, proclamations, and rituals devoid of love. They may not know *about* God, but innately from birth they intuit God as love and can sense love's presence when it lives dynamically in persons, institutions…and *us*.

36

Dialogue with a Hurtful Post

Recently, in the name of religion, patriotism, "fairness," and balance, I have seen social media posts that are inflammatory, hurtful, and divisive and often present snippets of material taken out of context and so are misleading. When seeing them, my initial thought has been, "How do I respond in a way that encourages the author to realize this type of post is only throwing more kerosene on the fire after so many people have been harmed already?"

When I saw a recent post from a person I like, I asked another wiser friend, "What should I write in response?" She responded, "I think you may be asking me the wrong question. A more important one I think may be: 'Will he really listen, and will it improve the situation in any way?'"

I didn't think about it too long because I knew the answer. "No," I replied. "He truly thinks he is being patriotic and seeking to show one group is as bad as or worse than the one to which he belongs."

After stepping away from the computer and conversation, I took a short walk and realized how sad I was about the post. When truly good people write posts that incite greater anger, divisiveness, and violence while thinking they are merely defending their position and group, the suffering they cause only seems to become greater. The comments that follow the post often bear this out.

I do know that a failure to act on my part can be cowardice and quiet, complicit behavior when evil reveals itself in support of a purported good. Yet, I think there must also be true discernment as to when to say something that would help and when to recognize it will only cause more verbal violence and lead nowhere.

I still remember seeing a post joyfully reinforcing a Catholic priest when he refused the Eucharist to a parishioner who was a politician who was personally against abortion but supported the law that said it was a woman's right. In the same post there was coverage of another priest who refused holy communion to an outwardly homosexual judge, and it included citing a canon of the church. In response, I wrote, "What about love? Will we be asked when we die what canons we followed, or did we love? Who are we to judge? We are not God." In response, some fairly "negative" comments were made.

After the interaction, I realized the responses about and to me were not really the problem. I should be able to shoulder such mere words. They really don't amount to much after seeing what people went through when I was working with helpers in Cambodia, Haiti, and Beirut and did the debriefing of Catholic relief workers evacuated from Rwanda during their bloody civil war.

What caused me to pause, though, was that my comment had the opposite impact of my desire and drained energy I could have put at the service of those professionals in medicine, nursing, ministry, education, social work, the military, and mental health whom I usually serve. I was simply irritating others and exhausting myself in the process.

Discerning when and how to comment on posts that you feel are leading to only more problems in your family, neighborhood, country, church, or the world is not easy. There is no simple key as to whether, when, and how to respond. However, I would caution against taking a stand every time you see a disturbing post.

At times it may be more helpful to the world if you hold your power. Share it instead only with those who have greater openness to learn that compassion is not fostered by inflammatory posts encouraging others toward violence, rigidity, and a lack of inclusiveness, *especially* when they are presented under the flag of patriotism, religion, family values, or a return to the "good old days" (that, by the way, often hid abuse, sexism, prejudice, and the abuse of power under a cloak of righteousness, at the expense of the poor, weak, and marginalized).

37

When Is It Time *Not* to Repeat Past Styles?

Which Made Sense Before, But Don't Now

I remember hearing about a woman who, after turning one hundred years of age, was asked, "What is the best thing about being the age you are?"

Her response was simple: "No more peer pressure."

In reality, however, for most of us it is not that simple. The interpersonal patterns of the past seem to linger—not only to our detriment but to the harm of those who deal with us.

I remember chatting with a noted physician who was totally amazing. In her specialty, gynecology, she was renowned. She was recognized by her peers, had written seminal works in clinical treatment, and had flourished both professionally and financially.

Now, it wasn't easy. She had come from a "traditional Catholic family" that had fostered her brothers' education and simply saw her as working as a secretary and then getting married and having many children. Since she was bright and desired to take her place in society helping others, she felt that while such a role was wonderful for some, it wasn't for her. In response, not only was her father but, surprisingly for some, even more so was her mother discouraging of her actualizing her abilities. The reality was she was much, much more intelligent and committed to a life of meaning and compassion than her brothers were. She was also a born leader.

When she saw me it was much later in her life—she had just turned eighty. As is the case with my individual work now, it was for *pro bono* mentoring for persons in the helping and healing professions who wanted to psychologically and spiritually turn the corner in their lives.

She told me she was quite happy but her interactions with others weren't as good as she felt they could be. Since she was so committed to making this a better world by being a guide for younger physicians, nurses, physician assistants, chaplains, and healthcare executives, somehow she felt she was missing the mark. "Could I help her?" was the request.

I told her I would do what I could and asked her if she would share with me some interactions that she felt didn't result as well as she wanted them to. She did, and then I did something unusual for me: I asked her if I could speak with several of those people. Rather than being resistant, she was more than willing—actually excited—about this idea. (You have to remember that she is a truly amazing person. We can be temporarily lost even though we are outstanding.)

When I actually did chat with them, they seemed

to have the same song to sing. When they interacted with her, the tone of her reaction seemed to be to let them know she was accomplished and would stand for no nonsense. It was as if instead of seeing them as younger appreciative colleagues, she was seeing them as her mother, as well as the sexist other physicians from medical school and the senior male colleagues she dealt with who were less proficient than she was but gave her a hard time.

When this tremendously accomplished physician and I finally met again, I shared with her their comments—both deservedly positive and the ones expressing confusion about the negative or ego-centered style she had when dealing with them. Because she is what I refer to as "a good soul," she was saddened by this and asked what she could do to fix it.

I told her that this isn't something that could be fixed. She needed to realize it was something that wasn't broken in the first place...and wasn't broken *now*. Her reaction appropriately pushed against her mother's original resistance, which was exacerbated by some of the pompous, threatened physicians she had to deal with at times. Now that she was retired and others needed her wisdom, however, to come from that same place as was appropriate in the past was now putting them off and actually preventing her from enjoying the freedom of knowing she was talented and blessed in so many ways. Instead, she was busying herself demonstrating her prowess and seeing younger, eager colleagues through the eyes of those who had demeaned her earlier in life.

I think all of us need to see this as we age. To constantly repeat in the present true challenges we experienced in the past is a waste of joy...our gifts...our ability to flow rather than fight with life. Recognizing and adequately addressing this makes a big difference in the years left in our own short life and increases our ability to make space for those who seek to walk with us through their own forest of challenges.

As a therapist and mentor, one of the greatest challenges for me is to let the patient know I can see the pain of the past but also let them know they are missing so much if they continue to live from that place in their lives that no longer is a reality for them. All of us must ask of ourselves, When is it time not to repeat the styles of the past that made sense then but don't now?

38

"What Are You Looking For? …Come and See" (John 1:38, 39)

What we look for is not necessarily what God is offering us. But if we do not "have the eyes to see," we will miss it. This is clearly explained in the New Testament on the road to Emmaus. Jesus's early followers were expecting the Messiah, who would offer power instead of service and compassion and a prayer that would reveal how we must challenge our own ways of viewing ourselves, the world, and God.

The result is, if we agreed to truly "come and see," we might find in Jesus a

- presence that is healing, welcoming, and encouraging, not divisive or dismissive;
- lack of defensiveness and harshness when questioned, but instead an absence of egoism;
- spirit of service and community, not power and glory;
- sense of love that would inflame our

hearts to find, explore, and share the gifts
we have been given as a person;
- willingness to recognize that success
and going fast is not the same as joining
together as a family so we can spiritually
go further;
- recognition that we only have a short
time on this earth and so stop denying
death and seeking possessions but become
more fully mindful to what is right in
front of us to enjoy;
- willingness to embrace gratitude in a
deeper way so we can rejoice in God's
gifts in a way that sharing them is not
a duty or sign of our generosity but a
natural outgrowth of our own abundance;
- lack of interest in others seeing us in a
positive way or thanking us for what we
do for them because we have already
been loved and given so much by God.

There is also more to see, of course, if we have an
attitude of openness and a lack of self-consciousness,
which often masquerades as self-awareness. Yes, it is
good for us to be asked again and again by Jesus, "What
are you looking for?" But we also must more fully
embrace the call to "come and see" by letting go and
being humble enough to *unlearn* so we can be empty
enough to receive new graces, in new times, so we can
think, feel, and behave in new ways.

39

Step by Step
…to a Balanced Approach
to Life and Others

Two young deacons on a pastoral assignment loved to meet for dinner each Sunday evening to share a meal and tell stories about what they experienced in the parish during the past week. One of the most enlivening parts of this ritual was to compare how their pastors would supervise them. Each had a very distinctive style.

One of the pastors was very detailed and organized. Supervision sessions were held weekly on a preset date, for a prescribed amount of time. They would carefully review the deacon's schedule from the past week and discuss how the young man had completed the duties set before him as a way to see what he had learned. The pastor would then make suggestions and offer corrections based on his years of experience in ministry. Hearing these stories, the other deacon found he could glean very helpful information himself, which would aid him in his priesthood going forward. He even took a few notes.

Following this, the other deacon would share the events of his week and comments made by his supervisor. His pastor's style was very different. Supervision sessions were sporadic and usually initiated by the deacon himself when he had gone through an experience that struck him for some reason. The supervisor, in this case, was more interested in the deacon's feelings and reflections rather than in outlining a "how-to" list. He was also quite spare in his teaching and responses but was able to get his point across in a few words. For instance, after one of the deacon's homilies, which he had prepared long and hard for in order to deal with a number of scriptural teachings and ways to apply them in life, he asked the pastor what he thought of it. In doing this he tried not to show in his facial expression and tone of his voice that he was quite proud of it.

The pastor's response was terse, as usual. He smiled and said, "Well, you certainly covered a lot of ground. You know a great deal and I learned some stuff myself from what you said in your lecture," and then went out to greet a few parishioners who wanted to meet with him.

The young man told his friend that at first blush he was pleased with his supervisor's response. But then the use of the word *lecture* and the phrase "you certainly covered a lot of ground" made him wonder.

"Did you follow up with him?" asked his friend.

"Yes, I did at dinner. I asked him again and pointed to the words he used.

"In response, he simply said, 'All of us can only take simple, single steps to meet Jesus, to do what is right and life-giving for ourselves and those we guide. If we give them too much, rather than helping them see the Light in measured ways, we burden them so they may become discouraged rather than encouraged. Since those in the pews are more highly educated than was the case many years ago, they will expand upon a single point made in ways we are not holy and wise enough to do for them. *Step by step* is what people can, and I think *should*, do in the spiritual life.'"

"What did he say after that?" the other seminarian asked.

"He said, 'Would you pass the roast? I think I'll have another slice.'"

The seminarian's eyes then lit up and he said, "You know, I am glad to learn from the other people at the parish office and your priest-supervisor on how I can be a better pastoral administrator. As a priest, what I *do* is important so I can make the most of what we have in order to help those in need. But, in my placement, I think Father is helping me also understand what it means to *be* a simple priest and to be more sensitive to the complex struggles of those with whom I am called to walk in life. I guess both approaches by our supervisors are important to learn so our life and ministry become balanced."

What the deacon was being taught was that a step-by-step approach in the spiritual life is not only enough for those we are present to help but a simple and powerful calling for us as well. God's grace often shows up more brightly in the daily efforts than in the broad, sometimes ego-centered, efforts that seek big changes rather than small, faithful responses.

40

A Hidden Fork in the Road

Recently, I received a Christmas card that had been returned. On it was written in bold black printing: **RETURN TO SENDER. RECIPIENT DECEASED**.

The man to whom I had sent the card was one of my former graduate students at St. Michael's College where I often taught in the summer. We had stayed in touch at Christmas even though I hadn't seen him since he completed his course of studies—some thirty years ago!

He was an outrageous fellow and fit in well with his ministry as a male religious ("brother") to high school students. He was bright, quick, committed, and caring and had a wonderful sense of humor. When I received the returned card and the no-nonsense explanation scrawled on the front, I felt a sense of bewilderment and sadness. I knew he had been ill and even suggested in the returned, unopened card that he feel free to email me if he wished. He had written a note the last time we were in touch, and I thought this would save him time and would open up the door to more frequent contact during this tough period in his life.

My first reaction to finding out about his death was to let the darkness of it envelop me. I find that not fully immersing myself in bad news leads only to denial and avoidance. It also raises the possibility of a distorted form of psychological and spiritual romanticism, which I don't find helpful. While it is true that I am pleased he is with God…I still wish that it weren't so soon!

As well as honestly letting it hit you, the next step is even more essential. It is to take a most helpful, often unseen, psychological and spiritual fork in the road: namely, to allow such a loss to eventually lead to receiving such beautiful insights as a greater appreciation for friendship that still exists in your life; a clearer understanding of your own mortality so you appreciate *each* moment as pure gift; and a more compelling impetus to be kind to those who cross your path by putting your own needs on hold for the moment so the other person might have the space to live more fully as well.

Hearing of someone's death can be horrible, and we need time to mourn the loss—and research shows us this period is longer than we had previously thought. It is foolish not to recognize that reality. Yet, there are also gifts that can eventually come from such dark events if we open our spiritual arms to greet them when the timing is right. The question for us, as always, is: *Will* we?

41

Hurtful "Religious" Posts

There is so much suffering in this world that lingers with me or that I choose to face in my work with professional helpers and healers going forward. The year of the worldwide COVID-19 pandemic, I was in Germany to speak to U.S. Air Force personnel. They were experiencing a 40 percent increase in suicides over their last worst year. Some months later, I spoke virtually to one thousand physicians, nurses, chaplains, healthcare executives, and other hospital caregivers, a recording of which went to 254,000 in their system. After that I gave a similar address to workers on a tuberculosis project in seven countries and then another several presentations to nurses throughout the country. In these presentations, the challenge is to be both honest and hopeful, as well as practical and inspirational.

To remain steady in my work with such good people doing great things but under terrible pressure, I look around me and seek not only to offer a healthy perspective but also to be grateful enough to absorb all the many varied gifts God is offering me. I do this with the guidance of a comment made by Pope John XXIII a long time ago: "Whoever has a heart full of love always has something to share."

Given this, it always surprises and saddens me to see some of the posts and reposts by religious people who share what they feel is a principle of their tradition that is divisive and rejecting and indicates that if you don't believe exactly as they do, you are not a faithful soul. The unconscious arrogance of the message is often closed with the statement, "I bet I won't get many 'Amens' for this post."

Now, in their efforts to be principled, the sad result is the unnecessary hurt they cause by their lack of humility and insight as to what they are doing. The point I often reiterate is this: When you take knowledge and you add humility, you get wisdom. And, when you take this very wisdom and add it to compassion, you get love…and God is love.

I know when people make such posts—and, worse yet, others repost them—they feel they are expressing scriptural values from the sliver they have chosen from the Bible. But even if they believe they are right in doing this, why spend the energy and space on doing so *now* when people need to feel love and a sense of community?

When I supervise clinicians and ask them, "Why did you say that to the patient?" their response often is, "Because I feel I was right."

I then broaden my questions so they can see the value of timing and pacing, as well as to review their own possibly unhealthy motivations that may be beyond their immediate awareness. So, I ask them further:

Why did you say this *now*?

Why did you say this now *in this way*?

And what did you *expect*?

When I did something foolish as a child, my parents would ask, "Why did you do that?" When I would respond because my friends were doing it, they would then invariably ask, "Oh, so if your friends jumped off a roof, you would follow them?"

When someone who is not self-aware seeks to be judgmental and self-righteous all the while feeling they are being the one called to be Scripture's angry prophet, they are to be prayed for in addition to those they have inadvertently hurt...not be given an "Amen" to what they feel is a just cause but is not based on love.

42

The Rabbi Shared a Secret

Rabbis are taught to help those who have lost their way or are seeking *the way* in their lives, so they don't miss it or the chance to help others not miss theirs. And this is at the core of the following interchange between a seeking soul in life and the rabbi we know as Jesus. He is asked a common rabbinical question (they were asked similar ones all the time): "What is the greatest commandment?" (Matt 22:36).

In response, he employs two classical rabbinical approaches. First, he responds by reaching into Torah for his response. Second, what he chooses initially puts people at ease, and when they feel secure, he pulls the rug out from under them to wake them up. To accomplish this he selects from Leviticus and Deuteronomy. He begins by selecting one of the heavy precepts of the 613 precepts of the Pharisees of the day and says, "You must love your God with your whole heart and your whole mind and your whole soul" (Matt 22:37). In response, you can easily image the person listening and nodding in affirmation of this. Yet, Jesus then reaches down and grasps a light precept and holds it up *on the same level* as the heavy precept: "And you must also love your neighbor as yourself" (v. 39).

In doing this, he is sharing the secret of life really: namely, that we must always balance presence to others, self, and God. We cannot be truly happy without being present to others. If done with a true spirit of humility and compassion, no matter what results, it will become a "circle of grace" in which we will receive as much, if not more, than we give. God comes to us through others in very concrete ways. Even people who are troubled find that when they reach out, new perspectives in life come to them. Second, we need to be present to ourselves because one of the greatest gifts we can share with others is our sense of resilience and inner peace, but we can't share what we don't have. Finally, the greatest presence is the specific attention we give to God. When this is lacking, we lose our way. We can even see it in those visibly committed to serving God when they preach doctrine without love, seek power without humility, and provide service only to those they deem worthy.

The rabbi we know as Jesus has long shared the secret of life in telling us to balance presence to God, others, and ourselves. During any major crisis, this balance is sure to be upset. But this can become a gift rather than just a bother. Major life interruptions can stop us from continuing our normal ways of living and remind us "where your treasure is, your heart is" (Matt 6:21) and, given our personality and circumstances, ask how we are balancing our availability to ourselves, others, and God in ways that will nourish our lives and spirit of compassion. This wake-up call may not be desirable, but since it is present, the question is *not* how fast can I return to a new normal? Instead, it is: How can I become more aware now of what is unconsciously stopping me from truly being present to a dynamic God so I can live my life and be compassionate in ways that all things—including *me*—are made new?

43

Turning to Peace…
and Lengthening the Distance
between "S" and "R"

Everyone has times of intensity in their lives and, hopefully, also times when there is a gentle rhythm and some quiet space.

Although I was on a modified lockdown due to COVID-19 and was at home most of the time, my schedule, peppered with virtual presentations, was still quite demanding.

In addition, I was preparing for several future virtual presentations and completing several writing projects, all the while attending to the usual tasks of life, including a small ceiling repair after a leak from a loose pipe. (I really think the devil was responsible, but I don't share that with everyone, so please keep it to yourself.)

Life is not lived in a vacuum, though, so amid all of this activity, the media was letting me know more graphically about a riot in the Capitol, a new strain of COVID-19 spreading across the nation, the extent of increasing poverty and inequality in America, and the screams of people who believed "My country right or wrong!" as they held religious symbols in one hand and handmade or purchased weapons in the other.

While all of this was going on, early one morning I saw a social media post attacking the newly elected president and an unfavorable comparison being made of him with the last person who held the office. Following this was a positive response to the post, referring to the new president by a belittling name. This was the *stimulus* (the "S"). Given all that was going on and what I deemed the foolishness of the premise and the sadness of the demeaning attitude, my immediate thought was, "Why would you post this now?...Why would you continue to name-call and foster divisiveness now?" This was my quick internal *response* (the "R").

Then, while I had allowed these events to cause turmoil briefly within me—a very short distance between "S" and "R"—I looked out the window behind my desk at the back of the house and saw the brightest red cardinal I have ever seen perched on the snow-topped fence nearby. After a few seconds he flew off, leaving me in a surprisingly more hopeful state of mind. And rather than responding to the destructive post that puzzled me because of its lack of sensitivity and kindness, I scrolled down and this time was greeted by another post with a totally different tone. It quoted St. Seraphim of Sarov as saying,

"Acquire the spirit of peace and thousands around you will be saved."

Continually seeking peace, a healthier perspective, and a better ability to have low expectations and high hopes of others, while also not adding fuel to the fire of people's fears, which underly their name-calling and expressions of anger and sarcasm, is not just an act of self-survival. It is also a gift to those around us who are often so troubled in these challenging times.

I think we must all recognize that psychologically leaning back from others' emotions and taking even a few moments in quiet time allows the distance between an unpleasant stimulus and an immediate response to be lengthened so clarity and peace can replace impulse, fear, and anger. The invitation is there for us from St. Seraphim…and God. I think we need to RSVP our acceptance of their invitation. When we do, some additional quiet time in our schedule will then enable us to take a stand from a stronger place of inward clarity and peace, rather than from a darker spirit that will only make things worse.

44

Replacing Spiritual Smugness ...with an Ongoing Fresh Awareness of Life and God

In encountering spiritual sages—either personally or through their writings—I am always struck by their openness to experiencing a dynamic God and, in the process, a life that evolves rather than remains stagnant under the guise of being a principled person. Such amazing mentors strike me by their willingness to entertain new possibilities and not be captured by the past, while still honoring sacred tradition.

Even their loss of a sense of certainty that may have buoyed them in the past paradoxically excites and leads them on. They believe, as did Thomas Merton, that "with deep faith comes deep doubt...so give up the business of suppressing doubt."

Preconceptions and habits can destroy such a spirit. It is also possible to be drunk on our intelligence or so-called spiritual achievements. This is deadly because intelligence and past accomplishments don't lead to wisdom without the presence of humility. In a similar vein, those who see themselves as "above" others who always view themselves as "beginners in the spiritual life" also miss the point of the ongoing search for God who is greater than our mental grasp.

The "spiritual smugness" that comes from worshiping where God lives (traditionalism and established religious practice or style) rather than the living God can also be dangerous to those we guide. Young people can clearly see the hypocrisy when persons (and those that follow them for their own "good" reasons) are waving the Bible while preaching and encouraging hate. This, in turn, rather than inspiring them to live more compassionately can have them become jaded and, as Maya Angelou once noted, "There is nothing so tragic as a young cynic. Because a young cynic goes from knowing nothing to believing nothing."

If, however, we are willing to model appreciation of our tradition of faith while being open to change and challenging the way we live it out in ritual and daily life, we will not only become more alive in the darkness but also more inclusive of others around us who are also searching for the Truth. We will be able to understand that the theological reality that anchors us now is good and spiritual harbors are safe, but at times we are also called to pull up our anchor and set out into the darkness on the ocean of faith to meet the living God.

As Annie Dillard wrote in *Teaching a Stone to Talk*, "You don't have to sit outside in the dark. If, however, you wish to look at the stars, you will find the darkness is necessary." The darkness may well represent the uncertainties of life, but the "stars" will also be there to encourage us to let go of what we now hold onto in order to step onto the water like Peter, so we can experience trust, fear, and the reality of the steadying hand of God. I think this is something worth remembering and praying about during troubling times.

One of the leading Jewish theologians and philosophers of the twentieth century, Rabbi Abraham Joshua Heschel, once spoke about prayer in this way: "Prayer is meaningless unless it is subversive, unless it seeks to overthrow and to ruin the pyramids of callousness, hatred, opportunism, falsehood." I need to remember that when I pray. What about you?

45

Rare Lived-Spirituality

Swiss psychiatrist Carl Jung once posed the question, "Where are the great and wise [persons] who do not merely talk about the meaning of life and the world... but really possess it?"

After meeting such a person, Matthieu Ricard, author of the book *Happiness*, seemed to have such a question in mind. His response was, "I'd found a reality that could inspire my whole life and give it direction and meaning." He had "met human beings who were enduringly happy."

I have sensed the same in the writings of certain persons, as well as personally in some rare instances. Their presence seemed brimming with kindness, understanding, and a wisdom fed by the combination of intelligence and humility. When this occurred, I knew it because I felt the calling not to impersonate them, because I had a different personality, background, and calling. But I felt deeply the need to imitate their deep commitment to Who and what are good.

Just as their paths were uncharted, so were mine. There would be no guardrails to steady my experiences going forward. Like the quest of the desert fathers (*Abbas*) and mothers (*Ammas*) of the fourth century, *ordinariness*, *authenticity*, and *purity of heart* would be the words to understand more completely, take more seriously, and embrace more fully. Self-importance, egoism, entitlement, and seeking to grasp life, rather than simply appreciate all it has to offer, need to be uncovered. They appear in many forms so as to fool us. Often they masquerade in such psychological costumes as self-respect, getting one's just due, enjoyment, and success. The "music" behind such deception is often the fear of losing out, being hurt, not being recognized or appreciated, and being needy.

Modeling attentiveness, serenity, graciousness, and altruism is the result of formation of an attitude that is self- and community-celebrating over only seeking security and self-satiation. Such an awareness through meditation and healthy friendship helps prevent us from falling off the road to compassion and joy. Losing our way is easy because the gullies of envy, self-debasement, or aggrandizement, and demanding the world be as we would wish it are so easy to fall into because others have done so and claim it is only right to be there.

Instead, the spiritual *life* that true wisdom figures live and model for us is free of such conflicts and struggles. It is a place of peace and a recognition that all things change that are *of* this world. It is demonstrated by having a healthy perspective and a response to those who invite us to walk with them by demonstrating such things as the following:

- our trust in them
- allowing them to pace their own journey

- the need to look at one's thinking and actions again and again to unveil the unhealthy attitudes that have stayed so long they seem to be true
- taking greater interest in ourselves but without becoming egocentric, which is not an easy pursuit
- simplicity, not being simplistic
- a desire to be both clear and kind in reflection so that, in seeing all our gifts, it becomes more possible to see how and when we trip over them in certain circumstances
- a willingness to recognize the great suffering in the world as a way to put our own travails in perspective

Finally, just as I would image my past mentors and those who have been enlightened enough to teach me by modeling compassion, when running into a disturbing or hurtful emotion caused by faulty thinking, hopefully others will image us when they are lost. And, as we have been lifted out of the prison of thinking and feeling what scares, upsets, or causes fear, they will sense our smile and be able to do the same.

46

"In the Middle of It All"
The Climb of Courageous,
Conscience-Driven Persons

Aperson came up to me recently and shared feeling very discouraged.

> I stand up for women's rights. In addition, I try to inform people that the poor don't have power so are often passed over and given excuses when they truly do need health care and jobs—which is not tantamount to my being a "socialist" or "communist." On the other hand, I also worry that people don't realize that abortion in the second and third trimester really is taking a human life and am attacked as being against other women's rights to choose.
>
> The result? I get tarred by "the right" simply because I feel we should follow the words of Jesus about welcoming strangers and taking care of poor people. They also tell me I am not "Right to Life" because I won't

object to women who have an abortion early in the pregnancy—especially in the case of rape and incest rather than simply "for convenience." They also make light of my being concerned about pollution, even though we are seeing more and more dying from it and soon there may be no turning back. They obviously have no sense of our responsibility recorded in the Bible in Genesis.

Then I get verbally beaten up by "the left" because I won't come on board to agreeing that abortion is all right *whenever* it happens—even late in the pregnancy with no dire medical reason for it to be done. Now, I understand it when people say, "Don't stand in the middle of the road because you will get run over" and why *reason, compromise,* and *dialogue* are seen as bad words now.

When she finished, she saw me smiling rather than looking concerned about what she had just shared. As a result, she looked at me directly and said, "What? I am telling you what I am going through and you're smiling." Then, after almost shouting at me, she leaned back and smiled in return at me. She knew me well enough from past encounters that I was going to offer a different view, a perspective that might open a door she could consider walking through.

After a few seconds of silence, I said, "When you climb a mountain that you must, when you reach the top it is not unusual to be out of breath. When you are courageous enough to seek to educate your conscience and not fall back on an easy out—to the left or right—then you pay a price for climbing that 'spiritual and psychological mountain.' If it has been a tough climb facing serious issues, then it is natural to feel discouraged. It is the very time when you ask yourself, 'Is it all worth it? Shouldn't I just stay at the bottom of the hill with the others?'"

In our subsequent interaction, my goal was to help her recognize that educating our own conscience and taking a stand based on what we truly believe is good is not easy. People who take a single issue and run with it, no matter how important it may be, no matter which side of the fence they are on, may seem principled, but it also avoids the complexity of life today. It actually is easier and, unfortunately, often simplistic—even if we say it is for religious reasons. Moreover, it can lead to a sense of being judgmental rather than leaving the ultimate decision to God.

Psychologically it would be interesting to reflect on the family background of those who would condemn those different than they are (homosexuals, persons with a different color skin, those who have had an abortion, or people who have difficulty speaking a second language). I still remember being puzzled by the condemning actions of a young person in ministry until someone who knew his family noted, "You've never met his mother have you? She is at every church service but will verbally cut another parishioner down at the ankles if she doesn't believe what she does."

When we are in the cheering section for those religious figures who seek to humiliate others who are "sinning," we need to look *not* at that person but at *ourselves*. I think we would find that if we were to confess our sins out loud, we would more readily see the real reason we might "take a stand" that is harsh, unnuanced, and hurtful of others. It is usually not for "religious reasons." It is often pure projection and a lack of maturity. It is a time to remember: "Whoever is without sin, let that person throw the first rock."

Softening our soul is not giving up on our values; it is living them out in love as we climb the mountain of conscience formation. The alternative to this is easier...*and more dangerous*. You and I might decide very differently about life than this woman. Still, like her, we must be willing to take on the challenge. When we let someone else make the climb for us, we will never be able to enjoy our unique God-given view from the spiritual mountaintop, and that would be a shame.

47

Who Is Your God?

When I have asked people who their God is, they have usually responded with a lengthy Scripture-based description. In addition, they have added how important God is in their lives. When I ask them what they think about when they wake up, what preoccupies them during the day, and what is in their minds when they retire at night, the answers are different from when asked about God.

I then follow up by quoting Jesus: "Where your treasure is, there your heart is" (Matt 6:21), and I add, "That is your God" rather than the beautiful description you gave me of what you believe God is in your life. What we must recognize is that we must be willing to see that our lives are often not centered on God enough to be living out of a dynamic spirit of faith. Instead, we are being led by unrecognized fears, unnecessary needs, and secular values, as well as by a denial of our impermanence and ultimate death, rather than from the heart of God.

Metropolitan Anthony of Sourozh, whom we know in the United States as Anthony Bloom, wrote in his classic work, *Beginning to Pray*,

There is a passage in Dickens' *Pickwick Papers* which is a very good description of my life and probably yours. Pickwick goes to the club. He hires a [horse drawn] cab and on the way he asks innumerable questions. Among the questions he says, "Tell me, how is it possible that such a mean and miserable horse can drive such a big and heavy cab?" The cabbie answers "You see, we have a magnificent pair of wheels which are so well oiled that it is enough for the horse to stir a little for the wheels to begin to turn and the poor horse must run for its life."

Bloom then comments, "Take the way in which we live most of the time. We are not the horse that pulls, we are the horse that runs away from the cab in fear of its life."

We must see how many false things have captured our hearts, have become our "gods." It is natural to become *concerned* about life's challenges. However, when we do it with the understanding of what we can control and do what we can, while letting others and God take care of the residue, it doesn't turn into worry. When we also practice a gratefulness that opens our eyes to all that is already in our lives, neediness doesn't have us constantly seeking what is "different," "more," or "perfect" so that we feel unsettled. Instead, with a grateful attitude we are able to see so much that moves us to joy and awe. With such an outlook, our compassion is not us simply giving to others but instead becomes an actual "circle of grace" in which we receive much more than we give, because we now have a healthier attitude and way of thinking about sharing.

In this way, when we are asked, "Who is your God?" we can answer by how we behave because our faith has given us the eyes to see, appreciate, and live differently than if we didn't have a God modeled after the Scriptures and lived in union with friends who also have a center of gravity that is spiritual rather than focused on secular values, needs, and philosophies.

48

Two Women…
Different Messages

A number of years ago, a pastor in Florida asked me if I would give a presentation on compassion, self-care, and prayer on a Monday evening. He said that it would be good if I could speak at all the Masses on the Sunday before as well. This would give me an opportunity to introduce myself and provide an overview of the presentation. In this way, the people would know what I would speak about in more depth the following night. Also, it would provide a core sense of my message for those unable to come for the full presentation.

After the first Mass on Sunday, I went to the back of the church to greet people as they left. During that period, a woman came up to me and said, "I wish you would have worn a tie since you were on the altar. It was disrespectful." In reply I said, "Oh, I did bring a tie to wear. However, when I went to put it on I realized that in rushing out of the house to the airport, I had taken the wrong one with me. It really clashed with my shirt and jacket and I thought it might be a distraction for people, so I left it off." To this, while looking at me stony-faced, she simply repeated, "I wish you would have worn a tie since you were on the altar. It was disrespectful," and walked away.

Later in the day there was the Sunday Mass held in Spanish. Usually, when an English-speaking person addresses the congregation, the presider, who was originally from a Spanish-speaking country, would then translate a summary of the comments made. I decided, however, to write out a few words that would capture the essence of my themes, have someone translate them into Spanish, and then have another person tape the presentation so I could hear how the words were pronounced, since I hadn't taken Spanish since high school.

After that Mass, another woman approached me—this time smiling broadly—and said quite excitedly, "I didn't know you spoke Spanish!" I smiled in return and said, "*Un poquito*" (a bit). It was obvious to me that she was very appreciative that I would at least try to communicate in her native language.

Occasionally the reactions of those two women come back to me in the form of the following questions—especially when I approach someone to give them feedback. Which one of these two women brought me Christ that day? Which one do I want to be like? In my facial expressions and that of others, how is God's message of love shared most deeply—even in passing encounters like the ones I had with these two women?

I think it is worth asking ourselves these questions, because we have no idea what people are going through when we are present to them...*even for a moment.*

49

True Self-Respect

When a fine work of art is unappreciated, senselessly defaced, or destroyed, there is great sadness and outrage. And when an undiscovered, previously forgotten, or lost priceless piece is uncovered or recovered, there is a stir of excitement and rippling of joy and gratitude among those who appreciate true beauty.

One of Rabbi Heschel's gifts was his keen awareness of these two realities in the case of that often unrecognized, fascinating living work of art we refer to as "the human person." Accordingly, a goal of much of his writing was to bring to light the possibilities of humanity by reminding us that we frequently miss being filled with wonder and awe at the sight of this central creation of God. He laments that we often forget that unique fragment of the divine milieu glimmers in our own selves: "Man sees the things that surround him long before he becomes aware of his own self. Many of us are conscious of the hiddenness of things, but few of us sense the mystery of our own presence."

He recognized that while we may give lip service to the special nature of the human person in creation, there seems to be a lack of full appreciation of the implication of our claims about the unique image that humanity ideally reflects: "Verbally we seem to be committed to the idea that [human beings are] created in the likeness of God. But are we committed to it intellectually? If the divine likeness is our premise, then the question arises: How should a being created in the likeness of God act, think, feel?"

Aristotle once said, "The aim of art is to represent not the outward appearance of things but their inward significance." So is it any surprise, then, that when Heschel was asked by an interviewer for NBC-TV shortly before his death, "What message have you for young people?" he replied very simply and without much hesitation or difficulty, "Remember that there is meaning beyond absurdity. Know that every deed counts, that every word is power. [And] above all, remember that you must build your life as if it were a work of art."

What he is urging is certainly in line with fellow rabbi Martin Buber, who wrote in his book *Way of Man*, "The Rabbi Zusya said a short time before his death, 'In the world to come, I shall not be asked, "Why were you not Moses?" Instead, I shall be asked, "Why were you not Zusya?"'"

For most of us, though, the route in life is not clear. We must search the deepest inclinations of our heart to see what our urges and talents are. Then we must not lose our way by pandering to what others would have us be and do. We must not forsake our own momentum in life for the call of others' view of success. Still, while this principle is straightforward, it is not easy. The poet e. e. cummings sensed this and summed up the tension quite well: "To be nobody but yourself in a world which is doing its best, night and day, to make you everybody else means to fight the hardest battle which any human being can fight, and never stop fighting."

But how often do we actually do this in life? Does this attitude constantly guide our daily choices, fire the flame of our deep motivations, and provide a theme for a continual sense of commitment to what is of true value about ourselves and the world, rather than merely what is utilitarian or might make us feel good for a while?

As we move ahead in our lives, it makes sense to reflect on the following words from Rabbi Heschel:

> Man has indeed become primarily a tool-making animal, and the world is now a gigantic toolbox for the satisfaction of his needs....The Greeks learned in order to comprehend. The Hebrews learned in order to revere. The modern man in order to use....We do not know any more how to justify and value except in terms of expediency....The problem of our age: denial of transcendence, the vapidity of values, emptiness in the heart, the decreased sensitivity to the imponderable quality of the spirit, the collapse of communication between the realm of tradition and the inner world of the individual. The central problem is that we do not know how to think, how to pray, how to cry, how to resist the deceptions of too many persuaders.

50

Faithfulness in the Spirit of Mother Teresa

At the heart of Mother Teresa's deep sense of faith were surely Christ's words, "I assure you, as often as you did it for one of the least of my brothers and sisters, you did it for me" (Matt 25:40). How was she so faithful, though? What were the elements of her sense of commitment that was so unrelenting—even amid terrible odds and resistance on the part of some of the people she served? Certainly among the elements were her persistence and "eyes of faith" that saw possibility even when there appeared to be none for the person she and her sisters were serving. We can see this in the following story.

"We have a place in Australia. (As you know, many of the aborigines live there in very bad conditions!)

"When we went around in that place, we found an old man in a most terrible condition.

"I went in there and tried to talk to him, and then I said, 'Kindly allow me to clean your place and clean your bed and so on.' He answered, 'I'm all right!'

"I said to him, 'You will be more all right if I clean your place.'

"In the end he allowed me to do it and when I was in his room (I call it a room, but it was really not a room!), I noticed he had a lamp, a very beautiful lamp but covered with dirt and dust. I said to him, 'Do you not light the lamp?' And he said, 'For whom? Nobody comes to me. I don't need to light the lamp.'

"Then I asked him, 'If the sisters come to you, will you light the lamp for them?' He answered, 'Yes, I'll do it.'

"So the sisters started going to him in the evening and he used to light the lamp.

"Afterwards (he lived for more than two years), he sent word to me through the sisters and said, 'Tell my friend, the light she lit in my life is still burning.'"

She was also a realist. She knew that "you learn humility only by accepting humiliations." Rather than being discouraged by them, she used them as a training ground for herself and the congregation of nuns she would eventually lead. You could see it in her even before she moved to Calcutta to work exclusively with the dying poor. For instance, when she was teaching at a school for girls, a terrible famine occurred in sections of India. She went out to beg for food for the girls. In response, one Hindu man spat at her. She took this without reacting angrily or slinking away. Instead, she looked at him in the eyes and said, "That's for me; now what about my girls." She reports in a matter-of-fact manner that not only did he give her something but that they became lifelong friends.

Her fierce compassion was tied to the art of letting go of her own ego. But once again, we must ask ourselves, how was she able to do this work? What encouraged her to be faithful amid even the most difficult of odds? Several things, I think. First, a love of contemplation. One of her famous sayings is, "In mental prayer, shut your eyes, shut your mouth, and open your heart." She recognized that "souls of prayer are souls of great silence. If you are careful of silence it will be easy to pray."

She also had a real sense of the purity of ordinariness. She said, "Our progress in holiness depends on God and on ourselves—on God's grace and our will to be holy. We must have a real living determination to reach holiness. 'I will be a saint' means I will despoil myself of all that is not God."

In addition, she stayed away from broad theoretical concepts about helping. Her incredible kindness was in the concrete. She once said, "Remember it is the individual that is important to us. In order to love a person, one must come close to him or her." She looked at people differently because of this—be they poor or wealthy. With respect to those who had nothing she noted, "The destitute who are dying...they are someone's children." Yet, when famous scientists who were visiting her asked for a suggestion on how they might live their lives in greater peace, joy, and compassion, she responded simply, "Smile at one another because we don't ever look at one another." She felt that "kindness has converted more people than zeal, science, or eloquence." She recognized that "thoughtfulness is the beginning of great sanctity."

From her prayer life and commitment to the will of God, she was also able to accomplish something that few helpers ever attain: a detachment from success—even from the work of caring itself! As a result, she said,

"However beautiful the work is, be detached from it, even ready to give it up. The work is not yours. The talents God has given you are not yours; they have been given to you for your use, for the Glory of God."

Her faithfulness also involved a sense of forgiveness that was dramatic. Otherwise, she would have been so filled with resentment at those who would allow such poverty to stand unnoticed. The image Mother Teresa used for true confession of one's sins is as a place of true love—like that of a child saying he's sorry to a loving parent and of being embraced. Such simple powerful images sustained her.

She also knew it was easier to hug the sad child than the grumpy one, to be more open to the problems in the persons closest to you than to ones you don't know. Yet, because of this deep connection between love in the concrete and her inner life of prayer, much became possible. To conclude in her own words:

> What we need is to love without getting tired.
> How does a lamp burn?
> Through the continuous input of small
>   drops of oil.
> What are the drops of oil in our lamp?
> They are the smallest things of daily life:
>   faithfulness, small words of kindness,
>   a thought for others,
>   our way of being silent, of looking,
>   of speaking, and of acting.

I would only add *Amen*.

Epilogue

~ *Gifting Our Inner Silent World* ~

Psychology and spirituality both claim an interest in our "inner life." This is no surprise. What we feel and how our outlook shapes our way of thinking, perceiving, and understanding determine so much in our brief lives.

Life is like a meal. Unfortunately, while our current fine repast sits in front of us, we often ignore it while silently remembering past courses or considering what we believe would be a grand menu to choose from in the future. And while this all happens, the meal gets cold, often remains untouched, and looks up at us like a sad, unappreciated dog, wondering, *Why would you ignore me?*

Furthermore, as we get older and the days seem to pass more quickly, we invent—or let others create—new projects that must be finished *before* our life can be as we say we want it to be. No wonder why death can be so surprising and even seem unfair. After all, we were in the middle of (yet another) chore and didn't get to the point of "enjoy," or even to the ability to lean back and smile broadly for a time.

Who dared sell us this way of existing?! Why, we sold ourselves this game of life, of course. We learned it well from those who came before us. And so that we won't feel as foolish as we should, we then surround ourselves with persons from the same mental tribe. In this way, we can have some fun together occasionally while taking a train of life swiftly moving in a circle rather than ahead.

Then, as proof that God's grace is true, we are given chances to meet some people who take a different path, a real spiritual *journey*! They know each day could be their last, and so they savor it in ways that a cup of tea actually tastes like a chalice of joy. Because of this, they also turn each person they meet into their final friend and aren't distracted by how they look or by future tasks to be done.

Such persons of compassion and graciousness don't count on, or demand, anything. They just live with gentle wonder. They are members of the "living communion of saints." You will know who they are when you meet them because you will feel more understood and at ease, yet clearer about your challenges, when you are in their presence.

And, because they are such amazing children of God, they also invite us to join them so we can experience the "kin-dom" of God, to sense life as everlasting by being alive in the *now*.

I think I'll join them. What about you?

Appendix

Experiences

10 Half-Minute (or Less) Reflections for Noontime

...Although Praying with Them May Take a Bit Longer

1. Strange Experiences with a True Mentor

The psychological prison camps we set up for ourselves are almost impregnable. Since the fences are invisible, finding a gate to freedom seems impossible. When we do spot it through good fortune, desire, or advice received, discouragement still reigns because initially it is locked by lasting defensiveness.

But then some strangely happy sages come along. Strange because they often own so little. Strange because they model joy in how they treat us and others whom they barely know. Strange because giving of themselves doesn't deprive them of their own life. Strange because they are so unlike the famous of this world who spend all their time shining on, but not really warming, our spirit with their graciousness and wisdom.

I am so happy when I "meet" such persons in their written words or encounter them personally. Such strange, happy sages remind me of what life might be when I walk with them and, when we part, know how to walk on my own more gratefully during the brief years we call "a life."

2. Mental Distance

I feel very far from some of my memories now. Most of the people in them are gone. Slowly and silently they left, often without warning. In their place I now have geese on the river and deer on the ground behind my house. Even a red fox comes occasionally, although by her speed and direction, my home is not her goal.

When we are in our heads with such reflection, we are alone and maybe lonely because we have interrupted our present experience with a reverie by closing the door to the gift offered us now.

3. An Orange in the Snow

Sometimes I put an orange in the snow to remember the color of a simple bright life, my life…and I rejoice again. It's not a choice. My smile can't help itself from appearing.

4. What Continues after Me

Knowing the river behind my house will still flow after I leave leaves me numb. But it is the numbness preceding becoming more awake…so that's necessary and nice, isn't it?

5. *Responsibility and Irresponsibility*

The responsibility to enjoy. The irresponsibility of coveting. I am always confusing the two of them. Still, gaining clarity would free me and set me apart because everyone speaks highly of freedom while preferring the cozy closet of a confined psychological life.

6. *Forgotten Angels*

As I am in a canoe gliding up a small river to the Perfumed Pagoda, the name of our destination reminds me of a caution Thich Nhat Hanh offered to compassionate people. He indicated that during the Vietnam War they were so busy helping the wounded that they tended to forget to also smell the scents of mint, coriander, and thyme that are even more prevalent in the countryside. Being someone who cares for others often results in our forgetting the "forgotten angels" (what is good around us, for us, and in us). This is foolish not only in terms of our own lives, but also such forgetfulness impacts others because we burn out and fail to model that, even in the darkness, there are points of light to reassure us.

7. *A Singular Spiritual Star*

Some people try to find you, get who you are. But you're not lost…just different, as God made you and holds you in the palm of his hand.

8. Sensing God's Presence

A foreign structure and sound greeted me as I approached Martha's Vineyard. As the ferry pulled in toward the dock, I could see the lighthouse. There are no lighthouses in the borough of Queens in the city of New York where I lived. At night I could also hear the foghorn, which signaled the need to take extra care. Something I didn't experience in my hometown, Maspeth. Both were strange encounters for me. Yet, both struck an unconscious chord, an archetype of warmth, compassion, being tucked in the safety of my home. What are your personal symbols of trust, hope, belonging, and love? If you look there, you may find God. Whereas the places you are looking now may be too mental and your mind too small to hold the magnificent *sense* of God's presence.

9. Questions

Our relationship with God is often presented to us as a secret assignation. Or you need the spiritual combination to unlock the gate of the secret garden. Or if you chant the perfect prayer at the correct cadence, the sky will finally open, grace will fall, and never again will you doubt the existence of God. The divine relationship is not a fairy tale, though; Sacred Scripture doesn't describe it that way. Instead, it is a relationship of awe, gratitude, and love. So the question is not what or where the key is, because there is no lock. The question is how can I love—myself fully and properly, others while expecting nothing in return, nature because of the story of Genesis it bestows on us, and more directly God? As this love leads me through an opening I hadn't seen clearly before, I walk into a garden I didn't expect or dream possible that fills me with only one question: How can I let God love me this way? This is a bigger question, and in asking it, we will stop wasting time on seeking little answers instead of realizing more clearly how God is already holding us in the palm of his hand.

10. Small Enough for Awe

When I was very young, I loved to lie on my back and look up at the clouds moving in the sky. For a while my eyes—well, I myself really—went along the rim of the earth with them. Then, I thought I would move above them…Why not? And, then I became an adult and it stopped. Now, I am much older and once again think, I'm small enough again…*Why not?* (I guess I haven't completely forgotten awe after all.)

A Final Personal Word to You

I hope the moments we have spent together have brought you little openings to new awareness, the appreciation of a bit of usable wisdom, and more compassion for those who are free enough to welcome your gift of presence to them.

My wish is that you also had some fun in opening or closing your day with the ideas, themes, stories, and hopes shared. If so, wonderful. If not, no worries. In that case, simply move on to other authors who are called to walk with *you*. But do it soon, don't delay or waste energy on being discouraged or disappointed in me or yourself. Life is too short for that.

The fact that you read this book in the first place means to me that God has already graced you with the urge to search more deeply and, *while doing it*, live more fully. Take care not to step on those graces by giving up or pulling back.

In closing, warm wishes to you on the *continuation* of this journey...*your* journey. I'm happy if you have been given the opportunity to go deeper *now*...for the present is all we have, and ever had for that matter.

About the Author

For over thirty-five years, **Dr. Robert Wicks** has been called on to speak calm into chaos by individuals and groups experiencing great stress, anxiety, and confusion.

Dr. Wicks received his doctorate in psychology (PsyD) from Hahnemann Medical College and Hospital, is professor emeritus at Loyola University Maryland, and has taught in universities and professional schools of psychology, medicine, nursing, theology, education, counseling, and social work. He was also the commencement speaker for Wright State School of Medicine and Stritch School of Medicine, as well as the commencement speaker for and the recipient of honorary doctorates from Georgian Court, Caldwell, and Marywood Universities.

In addition, Dr. Wicks has spoken on his major areas of expertise—resilience, self-care, the prevention of *secondary* stress (pressures encountered in reaching out to others), and the integration of psychology with classic spiritual wisdom—on Capitol Hill to members of Congress and their chiefs of staff, at Johns Hopkins School of Medicine, the U.S. Air Force Academy, the Mayo Clinic, the North American Aerospace Defense Command, the Defense Intelligence Agency, as well as at Boston's Children's Hospital, Harvard Divinity

School, Yale School of Nursing, Princeton Theological Seminary, and to members of the NATO Intelligence Fusion Center in England. He spoke at the Boston Public Library's commemoration of the Boston Marathon bombing, addressed ten thousand educators in the Air Canada Arena in Toronto, and was the opening keynote speaker to fifteen hundred physicians for the American Medical Directors Association. Dr. Wicks has also spoken at the FBI and New York City Police Academies; led a course on resilience in Beirut for relief workers from Aleppo, Syria; and addressed caregivers in twenty countries, including China, Vietnam, India, Thailand, Haiti, Northern Ireland, Hungary, Guatemala, Malta, New Zealand, Australia, France, England, and South Africa.

Dr. Wicks was responsible for the psychological debriefing for relief workers with NGOs who were evacuated from Rwanda during the genocide, and he worked in Cambodia with professionals from the English-speaking community who were present to help the Khmer people rebuild their nation following years of terror and torture. He delivered presentations on self-care at the National Naval Medical Center in Bethesda, Maryland, and Walter Reed Army Hospital to healthcare professionals responsible for Iraq and Afghan war veterans. More recently, Dr. Wicks addressed U.S. Army healthcare professionals returning from Africa, where they were assisting during the Ebola crisis, and he spoke virtually during the COVID-19 pandemic on resilience and self-care to thousands of physicians, nurses, and educators.

Dr. Wicks has published more than fifty books for both professionals and the general public. His spirituality books include *Riding the Dragon*; *Heartstorming: Creating a Place God Can Call Home*; and *Prayers for Uncertain Times*. Among his latest books from Oxford University Press are *The Simple Care of a Hopeful Heart*; *The Tao of Ordinariness*; *Perspective*; and *Bounce: Living the Resilient Life*. His books for professionals include works for physicians, nurses, psychologists, and persons in ministry. He is the recipient of the first annual Alumni Award for Excellence in Professional Psychology from Widener University; the Humanitarian of the Year Award from the American Counseling Association's Division on Spirituality, Ethics and Religious Values in Counseling; and the papal medal, *Pro Ecclesia et Pontifice*.

Also by Robert J. Wicks from
Paulist Press

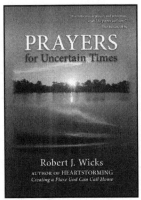

*P*rayers for Uncertain Times includes selected and new prayers, reflections, and dialogues all under one cover in a brief work that is easy to carry along during the day. With the conviction that a creative use of imagery allows us to surface a sense of God and self in a vivid and personally compelling way, Wicks also offers readers a straightforward process to write from their spiritual experiences and thereby embrace holiness in prayer and action.

He says, "When we pray and ask God to find us again in surprising ways amid the darkness, the portal to a transformed Divine relationship is seen in new ways under different circumstances. And, accordingly, how we live our life going forward is made new. *All things are made new*. With true prayer, nothing less than this should be sought and much more than this is possible." Author Robert Wicks desires through *Prayers for Uncertain Times* to offer hope, encouragement, and direction in the uncertain times in which we live.

Heartstorming was awarded first place among spirituality books for excellence in publishing in 2021 by the Association of Catholic Publishers and received a commendation from the Catholic Media Association in its contemporary spirituality book awards, also in 2021.

Heartstorming: Creating a Place God Can Call Home provides a point of entry to the contemplative life for anyone who will become or remain open to the movements of God in their daily life. The author's forty-five field notes show what can result if the reader takes a journey of growth in being spiritually directed and then goes on to write field notes by using the simple process Wicks makes available.

Through his own experience of God's nearness and drawing from his deep understanding of the human condition, Robert Wicks puts within reach of us all a healthy spiritual perspective as part of everyday living. Dr. Wicks writes convincingly and in practical terms, giving guidance to both the spiritually adventurous and weary souls among us. In all, he emphasizes the importance of listening to the inner life—mind, will, and emotions—on our way to an increasingly fresh engagement with God's will and purposes in and around us.

Related Books by Robert J. Wicks

Prayers for Uncertain Times

Heartstorming: Creating a Place God Can Call Home

Living a Gentle, Passionate Life

After 50

Handbook of Spirituality for Ministers,
Volumes 1 and 2 (Editor)

Prayer in the Catholic Tradition: A Handbook of
Practical Approaches (Editor)

Conversations with a Guardian Angel: A Novel

No Problem: Turning the Next Corner in the Spiritual Life

Availability: The Problem and the Gift

Prayerfulness

Everyday Simplicity

Riding the Dragon

Touching the Holy

Simple Changes

Night Call: Embracing Compassion and
Hope in a Troubled World

The Tao of Ordinariness: Humility and
Simplicity in a Narcissistic Age

Perspective: The Calm within the Storm

Bounce: Living the Resilient Life

The Resilient Clinician

The Inner Life of the Counselor

A Primer on Posttraumatic Growth